HOW
TO GET
OUT OF
{DEBT
and into Praise.

REV. JAMES T. MEEKS

HOW
TO GET
OUT OF
{DEBT

and into Praise.

MOODY PRESS
CHICAGO

© 2001 by
JAMES T. MEEKS

All Scripture quotations, unless otherwise indicated, are taken from the King James Version.

Library of Congress Cataloging-in-Publicaton Data

Meeks, James T., 1956–
    How to get out of debt--and into praise "God's plan for your financial freedom"/
James T. Meeks.
        p. cm.
    Includes bibliographical references.
    ISBN 0-8024-2993-9
        1. Finance, Personal--Religious aspects--Christianity. I. Title.

HG179 .M398 2001
332.024--dc21

2001030882

5 7 9 10 8 6 4

Printed in the United States of America

To my parents, James and Esther Meeks, without your love, tutoring, and mentoring I would not have come to know Jesus Christ as my personal Savior. As I look around at the things that have been accomplished through God, Salem Baptist Church, my many travels and associations, etc., I know I owe it all to you.

I thank my wife, Jamell, for her much needed love, support, and standing by my side in the good times as well as the bad. Jamell, next to God, you are my one and only love. Thank you for giving me the gift of our four children, Jamie, Janet, James Jr., and Jasmine, they all are my precious gems.

Thank you Lord, for your goodness, mercies, and grace that have brought me through thus far . . .

CONTENTS

OUR DIRTY LITTLE SECRET, GOD'S REDEEMING PLAN

OUR DIRTY LITTLE SECRET, GOD'S REDEEMING PLAN

If you're reading this book right now, then you are likely concerned about your financial future. Maybe you are concerned to the point that you realize you cannot undo the damage that has been done. You realize that you need help, supernatural help, to turn your situation around.

The wisest people are those who realize that God has a place in every aspect of their lives. Not just the Sunday-morning places. God has something to say about your financial life as well as your spiritual life. Consider, for example, Solomon's observation in Proverbs 13:11: "Wealth gotten by vanity shall be diminished: but he that gathereth by labour shall increase." Long before Merrill Lynch or Charles Schwab hit the scene, God had His people on the job dishing out practical financial counsel.

The good news is that God wants you free from debt, and the better news is that freedom from debt means freedom to serve God even more. Liberated from crippling worries about "How am I going to pay this bill?" or "How am I going to afford that increase in rent?" we are released to see God for who He is. We will have a view that is not obstructed by our material concerns.

Some readers might protest, "What does a preacher have to tell me about getting out of debt or handling my money? Isn't he stepping outside his boundaries? Stick to the preaching, Preacher." But when I present this message to people, it's not so much as a money expert than as a spiritual leader. You see, money *is* a spiritual issue. Jesus warned His followers that they could not serve both God and money (Matthew 6:24). And the apostle Paul wrote that the love of money is at the root of all kinds of evil (1 Timothy 6:10).

The Bible is a real-life book. It is about real people and real circumstances. Many people today think that the Bible is an abstract collection of writings. They think that the Bible is about a whole bunch of stuff that either happened way back then or that's going to happen in the future. The average person does not attach present-day relevance to the Bible. A recent Gallup poll found that 65 percent of Americans agree that the Bible "answers all or most of the basic questions of life." Unfortunately, this belief does not always seem to play itself out on the street: The poll goes on to note that only 37 percent of Americans actually read the Bible at least once a week.[1]

If we would just read the Bible, we would discover that it is more than an antiquated piece of mythology; it's a *now* book. It's not just about God then or God later, it's about the eternal God who is the same yesterday, today, and forever. And if God is the same yesterday, today, and forever, then whatever we discover about God yesterday also applies to God today. Whatever He did yesterday, He can do today and tomorrow. He is a God who is not constrained by the limitations of time.

As we study the Bible, one thing we will discover is that He has always wanted His people out of debt. People come to church week after week carrying a great weight. Nobody knows it, but the bills are worrying them to the point of depression. Day after day they are burdened by that mountain of debt. Their credit rating seems irreparably damaged. There seems to be no way out. But they cannot talk about it. It's too embarrassing.

We try to hide it deep down inside us and put on a good face for our friends and neighbors. But the nagging reality of debt is still there. We know it. God knows it. And God's Holy Spirit, in various ways, is warning us, compelling us to get out of it; to get our inner life in line with the outer face that we so bravely wear.

God will never leave you nor forsake you. But have you noticed that debt is in no big hurry to leave you either? You can't hope it away. You can't wish it away. You can't shoo it away like you would a mosquito. You can't get rid of your bills simply by acting like they are not there. I've heard many stories of people who, when they find a bill in the mailbox, simply don't open the envelope. Others won't even remove the mail from the box.

We think that the church is not a place to discuss bills and debt. And so we have come to use it as a safe haven, a place to get away from our problems for a little while. We come to church to "get our praise on." We sing and shout and jump for joy because there, for at least a couple of hours in the week, we can forget about it all. We can celebrate because the creditor isn't there, the phone isn't going to ring, and the collection agency is not going to bother us. So, in a way, the church has become our Noah's ark—our refuge from the maelstroms of debt.

But when you get through jumping for joy, when you get through waving your troubles away and get in your car to drive home, you've still got a car note you can barely pay. Last month's Visa bill is still overdue. I don't care if you shout in church. I don't care how excited you get about worshiping God. You're still in debt. Your relief was only temporary.

We've convinced ourselves that God is not concerned with stuff like debt. We think that God has to take care of more important stuff like getting people saved, raising the sun every day, and keeping the moon in the sky and oxygen in the air. We think that God is concerned with deep, "spiritual" stuff like who's speaking in tongues, who got baptized in Jesus' name, and to what denomination we belong. But did you know that the Bible says more about God's canceling debt than it does about His opening blinded eyes? That the Bible says more about canceling debt than it does about speaking in tongues? That the Bible says more about canceling debt than it does about what denomination you should belong to? If you're a believer, you need to get this next concept into your head. You need to start believing it. Even more important, you need to start living it: *God wants all of His people to live debt-free lives.*

If the power of debt-free living is going to flow in your life, if you are going to start becoming an individual who gets out of debt, it will start when you recognize that God is a God who cancels debt. You have to believe it. You must have the foresight to see it happening. You cannot walk around saying, "I'm broke, and I'm never going to get out of debt." That is the devil's lie. If you speak that way, you're always going to be broke. You will stay mired down in debt. But if you start seeing and believing, God will guide you into financial freedom.

We believe in God for everything else. We need to start believing that He can work in this area as well. He is not so busy or so holy that He's not concerned about our financial condition. And no, this is not a "name it and claim it" theology. This is a God who has every hair on your head numbered, a God who keeps track of the comings and goings of each wild creature. This is a God who cares about every facet of your life. And money, which can mess us up in so many ways, is definitely something that He is concerned about in our lives.

So you say, "Pastor Meeks, you don't understand. You don't know how big my mountain of bills is. I owe everybody."

Perhaps. But read Jeremiah 32:17. "Ah, Lord GOD! behold, thou hast made the heaven and the earth by thy great power and stretched out arm, and there is nothing too hard for thee." We always think that God has never seen a situation like ours. The truth is, God knew your situation before you did. Did Jeremiah 32 say there are some things that God can do and others that He cannot? Of course not. It said there is *nothing* too hard for Him. Do you know that your finances fall under the category of "nothing"? Do you know that your debt falls under that category?

In 1998, I presented a series of four sermons to my congregation at Salem Baptist Church of Chicago. The series was entitled "Debt Free in 2003." The objective was to provide a biblical and practical plan for helping people get out of debt in five years or less. When I began, I was not sure how the series would be received. But that week I was inundated with letters and phone calls. And since our services are broadcast on radio and TV, it wasn't just from folks in my congregation. People on the street thanked me. Person after person told me the same thing. They said, "Reverend Meeks, that sermon last Sunday—that was exactly what I needed!"

I knew money management was a problem for many people, but I had no idea until I preached the first message that so many believers were struggling with debt. But I was quickly schooled.

As the series progressed, I heard stories of how people were putting the principles into action. Just a few months after the series, I heard stories of how people had already improved their financial situations and were well on their way to climbing out of the debt pit. Some of the stories were simple accounts of how families made small changes in their finances and saw immediate improvements. Other reports were dramatic testimonies of how God had used the messages to miraculously lift people out of hopeless money predicaments.

I realized that when people truly embrace God's principles for getting out of debt, it's a life-changing event. And the wonderful thing is that it's simply an application of what God says in His Word.

That sermon series made such a difference in so many lives that we decided to expand it and record it in book form—and you're holding it right now. In these pages you will meet people from the Bible and from contemporary America. These are people who, for various reasons, seemed trapped in a hopeless quagmire of indebtedness. But they all had one thing in common—they received and believed God's promises about canceling debt. They discovered firsthand that God can do miraculous things in our financial lives if we will just hand over the anxiety (and credit cards) to Him.

I don't care how much you owe. I don't care to whom you owe. I don't care how long you've owed them. I don't care that you know people who are in the same situation as you and they never got out of it. I am here to tell you that if you have accepted Jesus Christ as your personal Savior, you are a child of God—that same God who made the heavens, that same God who made the earth, that same God to whom the cattle on the thousand hills belong. Regardless of your situation, nothing is too hard for God.

NOTE

1. "Six in Ten Americans Read the Bible at Least Occasionally," Gallup News Service, 20 Oct. 2000.

CHAPTER 1

OUT OF HOPELESSNESS: IT STARTS IN YOUR HOUSE

OUT OF HOPELESSNESS: IT STARTS IN YOUR HOUSE

I f there is someone with you in the room as you're beginning this chapter, turn to that person and say: "Neighbor, God wants you out of debt and into praise." If you're alone, then repeat this to yourself: "God wants me out of debt and into praise."

It's true. God wants you to get out of debt and into a lifestyle of service and worship. Did you ever notice how difficult it is to give God your full attention when you're fretting about this bill or that finance charge? Liberation from worldly entanglements is liberation to give God your full self. The more you start speaking this and believing it, the closer you will be to debt-free living.

Perhaps the most important thing to know right now as we begin this journey is that *God has canceled debt before.* Debt cancellation is nothing new for Him. Indeed, the very foundation of the Christian faith is based on the fact that God forgave our debt of sin through the sacrifice of His Son, Jesus Christ. But God was in the debt-forgiveness business long before that supreme event. In fact, we can go all the way back to the Old Testament to see His record on the matter. Look at 2 Kings 4.

> *Now there cried a certain woman of the wives of the sons of the prophets unto Elisha, saying, Thy servant my husband is dead; and thou knowest that thy servant did fear the LORD: and the creditor is come to take unto him my two sons to be bondmen. (2 Kings 4:1)*

Elisha was the protégé and successor of the great prophet Elijah. They served the nation of Israel as spiritual leaders during a dark period in the wake of King Solomon's reign, when the kingdom had been split into two and weakened by a series of bad kings. Once a mighty and unified nation, Israel was now the object of frequent invasions from foreign armies.

Though they were both heroic men of God and their names were similar, Elijah and Elisha were quite different in the way they operated. Elijah battled a king and the priests of Baal in spectacular confrontations of spiritual power. He separated himself from everyday folks and preached fiery messages of judgment that demanded repentance.

Elisha, on the other hand, lived among the common people. He made it his business to hang with down-and-out folks. As a preacher, his primary message was one of grace, mercy, and hope. So it was not unusual for a poor, distraught woman to come to him in search of assistance.

Before we go any further, there is an important point that should be underscored in this passage. This "certain woman" is a widow. If you are a widow who is in debt, understand that God cares about you. If you have fallen on hard times through no fault of your own, know that God is aware of your situation and that He is merciful. Even if it was your fault, God is still on your side. He has a special concern for the needy among us.

This particular widow's late husband was apparently one of Elisha's associate prophets. Then, like today, ministry was not a lucrative career, so this prophet's family was already poor. His death simply plunged the family into deeper financial crisis.

It's possible that the associate prophet had borrowed money or goods to support his wife and sons, perhaps to keep a family farm running. This would not have been out of the question for a man of God in that day. The Mosaic Law encouraged the practice of lending (Deuteronomy 15:7–8; Psalm 37:26; Matthew 5:42), and by extension made allowance for the practice of borrowing. The system included various checks and balances designed to keep lenders honest and borrowers from accumulating massive amounts of debt. For instance, lenders were discouraged from charging excessive interest (Proverbs 28:8; Ezekiel 18:8, 13). And every seventh year, the financial obligations of all individuals who were members of the nation of Israel were canceled. More on that later, but now, back to the widow.

Certainly the widow's husband was not expecting to die before paying off his debt. But he did, leaving the burden to his family. Today, one would hopefully have life insurance and a will in place to ensure the financial stability of the family. That was not an option for this man.

In those days, the taking and selling of children was a legal means of collecting on a debt. And since mercy did not seem to be in the heart of the widow's creditor, her two sons were now in danger of being taken as payment for the family's outstanding debt. In desperation she goes to Elisha, who had been her late husband's supervisor in the ministry.

It's important to note that this woman had the kind of faith to believe that whatever trouble she was in financially, God could work it out. She didn't go to the bank; she went to the man of God. She didn't go to the pawnshop; she went to the man of God. Playing the state lottery never occurred to this woman. Some of us, however, are looking for worldly solutions before seeking biblical solutions. Some of us are looking for earthly help before seeking heavenly help.

Jesus said, "But seek ye first the kingdom of God, and his righteousness; and all these things shall be added unto you" (see Matthew 6:33). It is always prudent to seek heavenly help first. If you are God's child, and everything that exists belongs to Him, then doesn't it make sense to turn to Him first?

This widow was lacking wealth, but not wisdom. She went to the man of God.

A FAMILY THING

And Elisha said unto her, What shall I do for thee? Tell me, what hast thou in the house? And she said, Thine handmaid hath not any thing in the house, save a pot of oil. Then he said, Go, borrow thee vessels abroad of all thy neighbours, even empty vessels; borrow not a few. And when thou art come in, thou shalt shut the door upon thee and upon thy sons, and shalt pour out into all those vessels, and thou shalt set aside that which is full." (2 Kings 4:2–4)

Elisha, himself a farmer, certainly did not have the financial means to rescue the distressed widow—but he served a

God who did. And the widow understood this. She appealed to Elisha on the basis of her husband's faithfulness as a believer and servant. She said, "You know he feared God."

Elisha replied, "What shall I do for you?" more to himself than to the woman. Then he asked her directly, "What do you have in your house?"

Now, this is important. Whatever counsel he is getting ready to offer to help the widow out of her financial straits starts in *her* house. Write this down: *It starts in your house.* If you want to get out of debt, the answer will always start with you. Simple actions that you can start doing in your own household must be at the foundation of your plan to get out of debt. If you're not willing to do the things that *you* can do— usually practical steps that can be taken right away—then you will never get out of debt. It starts in your house.

The widow told Elisha that she had nothing at home but a jar of oil. He instructed her to borrow additional containers from her neighbors—as many as she could. In other words, she was to prepare for something big. Like this woman, you must prepare confidently. Your answer—your miracle—will be in direct relation to the amount of faith you bring to the task. Let me say again that this is not a "name it and claim it" theology, which wrongly turns faith in God into some magical formula to get whatever you want. This is a fundamental spiritual principle. Jesus said, "According to your faith, be it unto you" (Matthew 9:29). James said, "Yet ye have not, because ye ask not" (James 4:2). Quite often, our blessings will be proportionate to the scale of our faith. And faith is not a work that we do to somehow influence God to give us something; it is a loving, instinctive trust in our sovereign Creator because He first loved us.

Elisha then told the widow to take the containers home and shut the door behind her and her boys. This was not a throwaway line. Elisha's point here was that the woman needed to bring her family in on what she was about to do. They all needed to be in agreement. After all, something was at stake for the woman's sons as well—namely, their freedom.

If you're going to work out your debt situation, it starts in your house—not just with you but the entire family. You will also need to be on the same page as you target your problem. Getting out of debt will require things to be done in the house that everybody has to agree on and not fight against. So, if you say the family will no longer be enjoying visits to Burger King or KFC until all the leftovers are gone, then everybody in the house has to agree. I actually know of some families where the kids page their parents at work and tell them to pick up some Popeye's Chicken on the way home because they don't want Mama's leftover beef stew. This kind of routine will become unacceptable for people who are serious about getting out of debt.

Too many working-class families are wasting their money and running up their credit card bills because their kids want the latest Kobe Bryant gym shoes when the old gym shoes haven't even worn out yet. They've just got to have the latest styles. But if you're going to get out of debt, there will need to be some agreement in the house that last year's Air Jordans will just have to last a little longer. How many families end up buying new winter coats every year? If you're going to escape the debt trap, there will need to be agreement that everybody's coat will have to last another winter. If there is a rip in the sleeve, you'll just have to sew it up.

The bottom line is this: *Escaping the debt trap will require a family lifestyle adjustment*. It is impossible to get out of debt if you are steadily creating more bills. There needs to be a family-wide freeze on unnecessary spending. I understand that the protruding springs on your living room sofa are a source of great embarrassment (not to mention discomfort), but that old sofa will have to last a little longer. Just take a bed sheet and put it over that spring!

At this point, someone usually wants to say, "But, Pastor, that's humiliating! What are my friends going to think?" The answer is simple: If your friends are that concerned about how your couch looks or what's up-to-date and what's passé in your house, then they may not be the type of friends that you need right now. If your friends criticize you for wearing last year's gym shoes or if they regularly scan your house trying to figure out what's new, you need to say to them, "I'll tell you what's new—my set of friends!" When you're trying to get out of debt, you don't have time for materialistic folks who make you feel ashamed because your clothing or home décor doesn't match up to their "wanna-be" standards. In fact, these are the kind of friends whose influence will invariably keep you enslaved in the debt mind-set.

So the poor widow was instructed to involve her sons in her debt-relief plan. It was a family thing. There had to be consensus in the house. They had to agree together that certain things would need to be done in order to get out of debt. Then, with the help of her sons, she was to pour her jar of oil into all the containers she had borrowed from her neighbors. And, according to Elisha, there would be enough oil to fill up several containers.

AN ACT OF FAITH

So she went from him, and shut the door upon her and upon her sons, who brought the vessels to her; and she poured out. And it came to pass, when the vessels were full, that she said unto her son, Bring me yet a vessel. And he said unto her, There is not a vessel more. And the oil stayed. Then she came

*and told the man of God. And he said, Go, sell the oil, and
pay thy debt, and live thou and thy children of the rest.
(2 Kings 4:5–7)*

More often than not, when you're trying to accomplish
something positive for your family—like getting out of debt
—it will not be an easy process. It will take discipline. It will
mean sticking to a plan. It may be time consuming. It may
mean delaying gratification on certain things—or doing without them altogether. In the end, you may decide that it's just
not worth it, that it's too embarrassing, that you don't have the
willpower to stick to the program. But this is where faith
comes in.

Consider the example of the poor widow. Elisha had given
her instructions that, in the natural, didn't make sense. But she
didn't ask questions. She didn't ask for an explanation. Instead,
she left Elisha and did what he said. It might have seemed
strange to her; it might have even seemed uncomfortable to
her; but she did it. She knew that Elisha was a man of God,
and she believed in the God that he served. So she acted by
faith.

Let's stop right there. If you don't get anything else from
this book, know that you may have very well just discovered
the most important point there is. Everything that you read
in these pages will be worthless if, after you've completed
the last sentence, you don't act on what you've learned. *By
faith, you must take action to escape the debt trap, or you will forever
be in its clutches.* Whether it's this book, or one by Larry Burkett,
or Ron Blue, or anyone else, reading the words is not enough;
you must act.

Many people go to financial planners and credit coun-
selors in search of assistance, but after they've received professional counsel, they continue to treat money the same way

they did before. But here in 2 Kings we see cooperation between the widow and Elisha. In similar fashion, as you set out to escape the debt trap, there must be cooperation between you and God. When God shares with you principles of how to get out of debt, you must cooperate with Him—and that means you have to do what He says.

The widow, with the assistance of her sons, followed Elisha's instructions and filled up the containers until there was none left to fill. She went back to Elisha and informed him of this miracle. "I've got a whole house full of oil," she told him. He said, "Go sell the oil, pay your debt, and live off what's left."

I want you to notice that if the widow had only gone to get a few containers, she would have only had a small supply of oil. But she went and got a lot of containers, so she had a surplus of oil. Elisha told her to sell it, pay off her debts with the proceeds, and live off the rest, which reveals another important point: *God does not want you living from paycheck to paycheck.* He told her to live off the savings, to live off the surplus. Even the ant, with his tiny insect wit, understands this principle. Solomon, the wise king, observed that the ant "which having no guide, overseer, or ruler, provideth her meat in the summer and gathereth her food in the harvest" (Proverbs 6:7–8).

The ant does not live from day to day not knowing where the next meal is coming from. It builds up a reserve and lives securely off that. We should strive to do the same with our resources. But before that can happen, we must get out of debt.

YOUR YEAR OF JUBILEE

Of course, the widow's miracle bounty of oil is not the only example of how God cancels our debts. Faith comes by hearing, and we need to hear the Scriptures over and over again when it comes to this matter of debt deliverance.

> *And at the end of every seven years thou shalt make a release. And this is the manner of the release: Every creditor that lendeth ought unto his neighbour shall release it; he shall not exact it of his neighbour, or of his brother; because it is called the* LORD*'s release. (Deuteronomy 15:1–2)*

According to God's law, Israel was to be a special nation in terms of the grace and brotherhood shown among its citizens. None of its people were to be left behind economically. In Deuteronomy 14:28–29, Moses informs the Israelites that they were to set aside a tithe of produce—i.e., grain, wine, oil, livestock—for the needy people in the nation. Later, in chapter 15, he tells them about God's seven-year plan; the cancellation of debt every seven years was one of God's provisions for helping to keep Israel's less fortunate members out of financial binds.

On top of that, according to Leviticus 25, every fiftieth year was to be a Year of Jubilee, during which there was to be no planting of crops, and all land purchased or sold during the previous forty-nine years was returned to its original owner. (This was not an unfair requirement: The land had originally been equally divided among Israel's citizens, so this ensured that no family would become either completely impoverished or disproportionately wealthy.) What's more, in the Year of Jubilee, one's financial obligations to others were totally forgiven, and Israelites who had sold themselves as slaves were set free.

So, are you ready for your Jubilee? Are you ready to have your debts wiped out and to be set free?

Notice, also, that the Year of Jubilee wasn't just a matter

of having one's personal debts cleared—the Israelites were also required to forgive others of their debts. While this practice might manifest itself in different ways today, the bottom-line principle is this: *When you're not ensnared by debt, you are in a better position to offer grace and freedom to those in need around you.* They may be your debtors, your neighbors down the street, or the homeless persons in the alley downtown. Debt-free living not only gives you freedom to strengthen your own financial house; it empowers you to bless others. It's just another dimension of our overarching theme: out of debt and into praise.

LIVING UNDER AN OPEN HEAVEN

Then Peter opened his mouth, and said, Of a truth I perceive that God is no respecter of persons. (Acts 10:34)

God not only has canceled debt before, but according to the apostle Peter, He also has proven Himself to be an equal opportunity God—that is, He does not favor one person over another. He does not have a clique of certain folks with whom He prefers to hang. He loves us all the same. He sent Jesus for each and every one of us. We are all equal in the heavenly Father's economy.

God's promises are not just for the widow who sought Elisha. They are not just for the people of Israel during the Year of Jubilee. Through Jesus Christ, God's promises are for all of us. His desire is that each of us would be free from the bondage of debt—both the spiritual and the financial kind.

The LORD shall open unto thee his good treasure, the heaven to give the rain unto thy land in his season, and to bless all the work of thine hand: and thou shalt lend unto many nations, and thou shalt not borrow. And the LORD shall make thee the head, and not the tail; and thou shalt be above only, and thou shalt not be beneath; if that thou hearken unto the commandments of the LORD thy God, which I command thee this day, to observe and to do them. (Deuteronomy 28:12–13)

We need to realize the plan that God has always had for His people. God wants us in a certain position because we belong to Him. If we are believers, we represent God to the world. In the Old Testament, it was Israel. In the New Testament, and today, it is His church. As the body of Christ, we are God's ambassadors to the world. And God does not want His ambassadors crippled by debt. He wants us in a position where we can bless others. God does not want us borrowing and borrowing, spending and spending. He wants us in a position where we can lend our resources —*His* resources—to others.

If you're going to represent God, doesn't it make sense for you to be pumping money into churches and charities and needy people's lives rather than adding to MasterCard's or Visa's fortunes? God wants you in a position where you can buy somebody else's lunch sometime. He wants you to be in a position to put gas into somebody else's car sometime. He wants you to be able to help somebody else with his rent sometime.

Of course, I'm not saying that all believers should be rich in material wealth. We live in a fallen world, and poverty is a reality of our sinful condition. We know from Deuteronomy 15:4 that God's desire is that there would be no poor people. But we also know from Deuteronomy 15:11 that God recognizes that sin inevitably creates inequality in the world. Jesus Himself said, "For ye have the poor always with you" (Matthew 26:11). Not all believers are going to be in a position to give freely of their financial resources. But we all can give something. God expects those of us who can give financially to be His earthly vehicle to assist the needy ones in our midst.

When you are constantly carrying around a load of debt, you cannot be the kind of servant God would like you to be. Deuteronomy 28:13 says that God wants to make His people the head and not the tail. Deuteronomy 28:12 says that God will open up the heavens to shower His blessings upon us. And why? So we can give to others.

Everything belongs to God. There is nothing that is not His. The silver is His and the gold is too. God is just looking for somebody He can trust, somebody who will brag on Him. God is just looking for somebody who will bless His name; somebody who will be faithful with what has been entrusted to him. God will give you stuff so that you can be a lender and not a borrower, but He cannot do it unless you are operating under an open heaven. Consider this with me: God opens up heaven to funnel us His riches. This means if you're ever going to get out of debt, you've got to learn how to operate under an open heaven. God cannot give you stuff if heaven is not open.

"So Pastor," you say, "how do I operate under an open heaven? What is it that I have to do in order to get heaven to open up?"

First of all, never lose sight of this: When you wake up in the morning, isn't heaven open? When you see that your children are healthy and your family is well fed, isn't heaven open? When you get your paycheck, isn't heaven open? When you get a refund from the IRS, isn't heaven open?

The answer to each of these questions is yes. But the book of Malachi shows us that there's a bit more to it than that.

Bring ye all the tithes into the storehouse, that there may be meat in mine house, and prove me now herewith, saith the Lord of hosts, if I will not open you the windows of heaven, and pour you out a blessing, that there shall not be room enough to receive it. (Malachi 3:10)

In a sense, heaven is open to us every day. There are general revelations of God's blessings and faithfulness all around us. Indeed, He rains on the just and unjust all the same. But how do we get God to swing open the "windows of heaven" even wider? The answer is, we must make Him Number One on our list. We must return to Him what is rightfully His.

God opens heaven when you give to Him first. When you share with God first, He opens up the heavens for you. And when He opens up heaven to the extent that He desires, He pours down blessings until we don't have any more room for them. And if we don't have enough room to receive them all, what does that mean? It means we've got something to share with others—and something to put away for the future.

Remember the widow? Can you imagine how that woman must have felt on the day of her miracle when she sold all those pots of oil, paid off her debts, and then was still able to live off her savings? She probably felt a freedom she had never known before. I'll bet you, every time she looked at her sons walking through the house she lifted her hands and said, "Thank You, Lord." The day that started off being the worst of her life ended up being the best. And why? Because she trusted God, and she was faithful in doing what He asked of her. She acted on her faith and was delivered out of debt and into praise.

If you're going to be delivered, you must start demonstrating that same level of faith. If you don't, you will find yourself perpetually living in the minus column of life—

always sending money out, never getting ahead. It is a slope that most of us find ourselves walking every day. And, as we will see, it is a very slippery one.

OUT OF EXCESS: SLAYING THE GIANT

OUT OF EXCESS: SLAYING THE GIANT

Will and Helen Patterson have been married for thirty-two years. They live in suburban Chicago in a pleasant middle-class neighborhood. They successfully raised two daughters, helped put them through college, and are now enjoying the peace and quiet of an empty nest. Will has worked for twenty years at a manufacturing company, and Helen has worked as a part-time nurse at a local clinic for the past five years. Now that the girls are gone, the Pattersons have begun thinking about retirement. But before they can do that, there are bills that need to be paid off. There's the roof that was replaced last year and the new hot-water heater. There's the car note and, of course, the never-ending mortgage. They realize that they have not saved much money at all. In the past two years, they have been scrambling to put money in a 401(k). Will and Helen, both in their early fifties, are more or less living from paycheck to paycheck.

Of course, there are times in all of our lives when we are forced to live from check to check. A twenty-two-year-old may have college loans to pay off before starting to build a substantial bank account. A young husband and wife may need several years before they can see significant progress in their savings or investments. Ideally, though, we ought not to be fifty years old and still just getting started. Wise stewardship dictates that each of us be moving toward a point where we can live off our savings. Implicit in the idea of living off our savings is the notion that we will have savings in the first place. That means we cannot spend every dollar we get our hands on.

Therein lies one of our culture's biggest problems—the joy of spending. Though things may be slowing down now, in general we are blessed to be living in an era of remarkable economic growth. However, in the midst of one of the most prosperous periods in our nation's history, when unemployment is at an all-time low and people are making more money than ever before, they are also *spending* more money than ever before. Worse, they aren't putting any of it aside for the proverbial "rainy day." Personal debt is at a record high, while personal savings are heading in the other direction. A 1999 study by the U.S. Commerce Department found that although our incomes have risen 5.9 percent, our spending has risen 7 percent and our savings has dropped to an all-time annual low of 2.4 percent after taxes. When it comes to money, we've gotten our priorities confused.

I could go on for several pages discussing how this society has corrupted our common sense when it comes to basic money skills. The African-American community, in particular, has found it difficult to escape the lure of spending with no regard for the future. A 2000 study by Christian pollster George Barna revealed that blacks are approximately 30 percent more likely than whites or Hispanics to be "in debt."[1] Professional athletes and rap-music stars, the primary heroes of our young people today, are seen on television and in music videos with sparkling jewelry, extravagant mansions, and lavish cars. Their images of excess indoctrinate many young minds with the new American religion of materialism.

On the one hand, many African-Americans are doing better than ever before. In recent years, millions of us have entered the ranks of the middle class—something that would have seemed unimaginable just a few short decades ago. Sadly, though, we have not handled these economic gains well. And there are too few voices speaking out to help us get our financial houses in order.

For too many middle-class blacks, the only "saving" we know is the kind that happens on Sunday mornings during the altar call, and "investing" is something that white men do on Wall Street. Meanwhile, our incomes are growing and we have nothing long-term to show for it. Instead, bigger paychecks mean bigger spending sprees. The sisters think they have to look fine and cute, so they waste wads of money on fancy hairdos, glitzy manicures, and shiny new clothes. The brothers have to be cool, so they bankrupt their futures to purchase Lincoln Navigators, deafening car stereos, and gargantuan big-screen TVs that are often larger than the rooms in which they are placed.

And by no means are blacks alone. As a nation, we are under massive pressure to "keep up with the Joneses." Consequently, debt has become our national way of life. According to national statistics, Americans, on the average, have about

$5,000 worth of credit card debt per household—and the average interest rate is 18 percent.[2] That could take more than five years to pay off. No wonder we're not able to save anything.

Ironically, our economy is strongest when more people are saddled with a load of debt. Alan Greenspan, the Federal Reserve chairman, whom many people credit for turning the U.S. economy around, skillfully manipulates interest rates in hopes of enticing more borrowing and, hence, more debt.

Our nation is driven by debt. But you don't have to let debt drive you. Remember the theme from the previous chapter? *God has canceled debt before.* And He can cancel yours, too.

KILLING YOUR GOLIATHS

And the men of Israel said, Have ye seen this man that is come up? Surely to defy Israel is he come up; and it shall be, that the man who killeth him, the king will enrich him with great riches, and will give him his daughter, and make his father's house free in Israel." (1 Samuel 17:25)

Whether they know the Bible or not, everyone is familiar with the story of David and Goliath. A brave boy slays a huge giant. The moral: Size doesn't matter when you have God on your side. True. But there's more to the story. Let's consider it in its context (1 Samuel 17:1–58).

In ancient times, wars between nations were often determined by representative combat—that is, a warrior from each army would fight, and the victor of the contest would, in effect, signify a victory for his side. It was believed that the outcome of the fight was decided more by the soldier's god than by the soldier's military prowess. The Philistines, a pagan nation, descended on Israel for such a battle.

In this clash, the Philistines' representative was Goliath, a nine-foot-nine warrior with a 33-pound spear, a bronze helmet, and a 125-pound coat of armor. He also had a hefty defensive shield that was carried by an aide. Goliath was ready to throw down. Like a mutant NBA player, he stood before the Israelites talking trash: "You want some of this? I dare you to send somebody out here!"

Saul, who was then Israel's king, was a fearful man who lacked confidence in God's strength. The Israelite army picked up on its king's apprehension and, consequently, was terrified to go against Goliath.

As an incentive, Saul had even announced an attractive reward for whoever conjured up the courage to face Goliath. The man who killed him would receive great wealth, Saul's daughter in marriage, and a tax exemption for his father's family—which meant relief from debt. Put another way: The existing and future debts of that man's family would be canceled.

Even with that enticing offer on the table, none of the men in Israel's army was prepared to take on Goliath. Finally, David, a young shepherd, emerged as the only person with enough faith to go toe to toe with the giant—and he wasn't even a member of the army.

You know the rest of the story: David, equipped with little more than a slingshot and five smooth stones, confronts Goliath in God's name and, with a single rock to the giant's forehead, takes him out.

With God, all things are possible. The weak are made strong. The poor are made rich. And the debtors are made free. With his slingshot and confidence in God, David slew the Philistine giant. With a little discipline and David-like faith in God, you, too, can slay a giant—the giant of debt. God has canceled debt before.

THE POWER OF GOD'S FREEDOM

Jesus answered them, Verily, verily, I say unto you, Whosoever committeth sin is the servant of sin. And the servant abideth not in the house for ever: but the Son abideth ever. If the Son therefore shall make you free, ye shall be free indeed. (John 8:34–36)

When Salem Baptist Church moved into its present home in 1990, we found a community suffering from urban decay, white flight, economic depression, and gang infestation. The Roseland neighborhood, on the Far South Side of Chicago, is not the most scenic locale. Vacant buildings dot the streets. The buildings that are occupied house pawnshops, currency exchanges, beeper shops, storefront churches, and tiny grocery stores encased in metal bars and selling more lottery tickets than food.

It's not the finest looking place, but it's my home. Not only do I lead a church there, my family resides there. And to me it's beautiful. I'm not just being sentimental when I say that. When I look at Roseland, I don't see what's there now. I see what it can be. I see what it's becoming by the transforming presence of God's people in the community.

Something you soon won't see in Roseland is a liquor store. That's because the saints of Salem Baptist Church decided to add feet and political muscle to our prayers that the community would be rid of alcohol. We committed to mobilizing the residents to shut down every liquor store in Roseland. Besides looking bad, these places destroy lives. My heart breaks when I see the hopelessness on the faces of brothers hanging out in the doorways of these places, or standing on the corners with nothing to do but drink from a forty-ounce in a brown paper sack.

Alcohol is one of the deadliest drugs in America's inner cities, maybe deadlier than crack cocaine. It robs able-bodied men of their productivity, wrecks families, leaves children fatherless and men and women jobless. We had to get this destroyer out of our neighborhood.

In 1998, we mobilized the residents of Roseland and the surrounding communities and led the charge against the liquor stores and taverns. Together, we got a referendum put on the local ballot to ban the sale of alcohol in our community. On Election Day, residents voted overwhelmingly to close down thirty liquor establishments.

The ensuing legal battle has delayed the closure of many of the businesses, but notice has been served. The people have spoken. The radical transformation of an economically depressed community can only happen by the liberating power of Jesus Christ. But God's people must be willing to add deliberate action to their prayers: to engage the political process, to march on the streets, to say the unpopular thing when it needs to be said, to abandon their comfort zones and put themselves on the front lines for justice, holiness, and reconciliation. Did you know that God often reveals His liberating power through the words and actions of His people?

Jesus said, "If the Son therefore shall make you free, ye shall be free indeed" (John 8:36). When you're a child of God, this should become the cornerstone of your new life in Christ. Nevertheless, many of us go to church, Sunday after Sunday, professing this freedom when in reality we are still in bondage. Bondage can take many forms—nicotine, lying, inappropriate relationships. But, for purposes of this book, let's focus on financial bondage.

Many of us are held captive by our finances, or more realistically, by our lack thereof. We hear preachers preach and teach about freedom in Christ, yet we think that this freedom is something reserved for our spiritual lives only. When we think of Jesus as setting us free, we only think of Him setting us free from sin. But the kind of freedom that the Son of God provides encompasses every aspect of our lives. Jesus' ability to set us free is not limited to spiritual bondage.

Since death and life are in the power of the tongue, let's reinforce what we've just discovered. If you're reading this chapter with someone in the room, turn to that person and say, "Neighbor, Jesus can and He will set you free from whatever enslaves you." If you're alone, make it personal: "Jesus can and will set *me* free from whatever enslaves me."

In the gospel of Luke, we see Jesus in a sort of a "coming out party" moment at the synagogue in Nazareth. Standing before the people, He recited a passage from the prophet Isaiah:

> *The Spirit of the LORD is upon me, because he hath anointed me to preach the gospel to the poor; he hath sent me to heal the brokenhearted, to preach deliverance to the captives, and recovering of sight to the blind, to set at liberty them that are bruised, to preach the acceptable year of the LORD. (Luke 4:18–19)*

Here, Jesus was not just ritualistically reading Scripture before the congregation; He was openly declaring something essential about Himself. He was, as it were, declaring His job description. Indeed, He went on to say, "This day is this scripture fulfilled in your ears" (verse 21). In other words, "You're looking at your Freedom!" Jesus is your healing. He is your deliverance. He *is* your liberation incarnate.

Jesus described His mission in both spiritual and physical terms. For Him, the two were inextricably tied together. So when we talk about freedom in Christ, it is not just limited to our spiritual destiny. It includes every dimension of our lives—including our finances. God wants you to be financially free—from debt, from overspending, from materialism.

OWE NO MAN

Render therefore to all their dues: tribute to whom tribute is due; custom to whom custom; fear to whom fear; honour to whom honour. Owe no man any thing, but to love one another: for he that loveth another hath fulfilled the law. (Romans 13:7–8)

In the last chapter, we saw in Deuteronomy how God wants His people to be lenders and not borrowers, the head and not the tail. A testament later, Paul concurs with this when he exhorts the church in Rome to "owe no one anything except . . . love" (Romans 13:8 NKJV). God wants to get us to the point where we don't owe anybody anything, where we're simply able to share our blessings with others.

I'm the pastor of a twelve thousand-member congregation. How would it look if I were constantly going over to the members' homes for dinner and other favors? What if I gathered my wife and four children and started at Deacon Adam's house on Monday and said, "Deacon, the Meeks family budget has been really tight. Could you feed us?" And then on Tuesday, we head to Deacon Brown's house and tell him, "Deacon, we're kind of down on our luck this week; could you loan us $100 to pay our light bill?" And then on Wednesday we go to Deacon Chamber's house and ask for gas money. Don't you think people would begin to wonder what's wrong with us? My congregation is full of wonderful families, so I'm sure they would treat us graciously. But later, they'd probably think to themselves, *Doesn't Pastor Meeks receive enough pay?* or *Pastor must not know how to manage his finances.* It would be inappropriate for me as the leader of my large church not to take care of my financial situation in a better way than that.

Likewise, it is an embarrassment to God when we call ourselves His ambassadors and yet we're going across town begging every financial institution for its money. We are, in effect, asking them to take care of us. Not only that, we've got the nerve to have JESUS SAVES custom printed on the checks with which we're paying them back! Isn't it possible that these people might start wondering, *What good is their Jesus if they have to borrow money from us all the time?*

DEBT-FREE LANGUAGE

For verily I say unto you, That whosoever shall say unto this mountain, Be thou removed, and be thou cast into the sea; and shall not doubt in his heart, but shall believe that those things which he saith shall come to pass; he shall have whatsoever he saith. (Mark 11:23)

How we talk about this notion of getting out of debt is very important. We will never start acting on debt-free principles until we start speaking debt-free language. What people say usually stems from the deep thoughts and beliefs found in their hearts (Luke 6:45). So, if we truly believe that we can be debt free, it ought to be evident in the way we talk. We have to start talking as if we believe this thing.

Jesus tells us about the power of a word spoken in true faith. In Mark 11, He says that mountains can be moved if we speak it in faith. Solomon, in Proverbs 18:21, says that "death and life are in the power of the tongue." You can bless or curse yourself based on what you say to and about yourself. Likewise, you can bless or curse others by the words you say to and about them.

Many adults remember years later some of the stern words their parents said to them when they were children: "You are stupid." "No, let someone else do it." "You are just like your no-good lyin' daddy." And so on. In certain generations of the African-American community, white and black teachers told many of us to " forget it" when we expressed aspirations of being astronauts or doctors or nuclear physicists. They said, "You can't do that. Why don't you focus on being a mechanic or a truck driver?" And for many people, those words stuck and influenced them the rest of their lives. On the other hand, many people are blessed to recall stories about a parent or teacher who encouraged them and inspired them to dream big dreams.

Death and life are in the power of the tongue. That's why we need to watch what we say to our young people, our neighbors, and ourselves. We need to learn how to speak positive things into other people's lives—and into our own. Our finances are one area where we need to increase the life language. Tell yourself, "I'm going to be debt free! God wants me to be debt free!"

All you may see today is hopelessness when you look at that mountain of bills, but you can tell that mountain to be gone. And then, with faith in God, self-control, and hard work, you can make it so. The giant might look too big to beat, the mountain might look too large to throw, but it can be done. Tell yourself: "Nothing is too hard for my God. The Son has set me free and, therefore, I will be debt free!"

NOTES

1. Barna Research Online, 2000, reports that 46 percent of blacks are in debt compared to 36 percent of whites and 34 percent of Hispanics.
2. "Controlling Debt: Top 10 Things to Know," www.Money.com, 2000.

CHAPTER 3

OUT OF DEBT—PART 1: HOW TO GET THERE

OUT OF DEBT—PART 1: HOW TO GET THERE

A woman that I'll refer to as Carolyn Jones works as an agent for a major insurance company in Chicago. She is a sharp businesswoman who obviously has refined tastes when it comes to clothing and jewelry. Her smartly styled hair and elegantly manicured nails suggest she's a woman who wants to present an image of professionalism and class.

Carolyn is the wife of a guy I'll refer to as William Jones, a business executive and one of my associate ministers. A wonderful couple, the Joneses are the parents of two rapidly growing teenage sons. No one who sees them would even suspect that this picture-perfect, middle-class family could be trapped in the throes of financial indebtedness. But pictures rarely tell the whole story.

"My husband and I make a lot of money, but we spend a lot of money," says Carolyn. "We had all kinds of loans—car, home improvement, you name it. In 1996 alone, we had twenty-three different loans and credit card accounts." Not including the mortgage and car notes, she estimates they owed more than $80,000.

Carolyn's problem, she admits, was that she liked to buy things: stylish outfits, lavish jewelry, new windows for the house. "I was a shopaholic," she says. "It made me feel better. It was definitely a recreational thing." It wasn't just things for herself. She also bought clothes and surprise gifts for her husband and sons. They, too, were in on the addiction. And that's exactly what it was. She and her family were addicted to stuff—and it was destroying their financial fitness.

"I knew that I was in bondage," Carolyn told me recently, "but it didn't really hit me until you started your sermons on becoming debt free by 2003. I sat there saying to myself, *Yeah, right. There's no way we can get rid of all our debt in five years.* But I wanted to be free of that bondage. So I listened closely to what you had to say, and my husband and I agreed that we would give your program a chance. We had nothing to lose but our bills."

The Joneses put the debt-freedom plan into action and discovered that getting out of debt in five years or less was a very realistic objective when they set their hearts and minds to it.

SETTING YOUR SIGHTS

When I use the phrase *debt free,* I've come to think of it as characterized by two levels. Ultimately, it describes being in a financial position where you can pay off your mortgage and car note and still have enough money in your savings account to cover your insurance and monthly utilities. I know that's a lofty goal, but we need to think big. This needs to be our ultimate long-term objective.

Let's think about it in weight-loss terms. You don't get from a size 18 to a size 8 overnight, do you? Of course not. There are the stages called sizes 16, 14, and 12 in between. You have to pass through those intermediate sizes if you ever hope to fit into the size 8. And usually the more you lose, the more difficult it is to lose. Oftentimes, you may get stuck somewhere between size 12 and size 10 and never quite get to the size 8. So it is with getting out of debt. Our progress may not always be as rapid or noticeable as we'd prefer, but we must keep going.

The goal is to get to a place where we don't have any bills. However, to get there, for many of us, we will need to set our sights on a more immediately achievable level. So for right now when I use the phrase *debt free,* I'm talking about how to get rid of the charge cards and the second mortgages and the furniture bills and the Sears and Marshall Field's accounts—all the bills that we have other than mortgage, car note, insurance, and utilities.

As I noted in the previous chapter, we live in a society designed to keep us in debt. Have you noticed that you don't even have to ask for a charge card. If you're living and breathing and have a Social Security number, it will usually find you. You can be at home eating dinner, and the phone will ring and there's a really sweet voice on the other end congratulating you for being preapproved to receive First Bank's Super Titanium Card with a low interest rate and no annual fee. What the person doesn't tell you over the phone is the fine print: The low interest rate will be quadrupled in three months and the annual fee will be activated in exactly 365 days.

If they don't get you on the phone, they'll get you in the mailbox. Every day you are bombarded with direct mail campaigns screaming at you to just sign on the dotted line for this or that card. They try to make you feel so special. Some of us see that we've been preapproved and we feel so proud. We see that Visa and MasterCard want us as one of their special metallic members, and we think it's a blessing.

But it's not. When we see the special offer from First Bank, many people celebrate: "Praise the Lord, my credit rating is A#1!" or "Wow! They've increased my limit to $10,000." Sometimes the card is already in the envelope, and all you have to do is call to get it activated. And, boy, is it ever a pretty card. It's all gold and glittery. But watch out! The devil may be behind that glittering piece of plastic. In fact, for many, it could very well be described as the devil in an envelope! You may not see the horns and long tail, but make no mistake about it, he's in there.

And no marvel; for Satan himself is transformed into an angel of light. Therefore it is no great thing if his ministers also be transformed as the ministers of righteousness; whose end shall be according to their works. (2 Corinthians 11:14–15)

Did you know that the devil often comes to us as an angel of light? He presents himself as something good, something that will help us live more satisfying lives. We activate the Visa Card; we sign up for the J.C. Penney account—after all, we can get 20 percent off our purchase that day just for signing up. It looks harmless enough at first. But then, all of a sudden, there we are like the Joneses—in financial bondage.

We have to know the truth. America runs on capitalism, and the success of the system depends on keeping us greedy as consumers. The more stuff we buy, the better off the economy becomes. The banks and stores know that we cannot afford to buy all the things we want, so they make it easy for us to get it *now*. But did you know that credit is just like sin? We can enjoy as much of it as we'd like right now—but rest assured, there's a payday down the road. We love to shop until we drop, but rarely do we think ahead to the day when the credit card statement will arrive in our mailbox and we will be forced to confront the consequences of our reckless behavior.

TEN STEPS TO DEBT FREEDOM

So how do we get to the point where we eliminate all of our bills except the big ones: mortgage, car note, insurance and utilities? Here's the plan that has helped William and Carolyn Jones—and many other families—reclaim their financial freedom.

1. Pray. As you would suspect, the undergirding principle in our plan is to invite God into the program. It's only through His power that you will find the ability to do battle with the spiritual forces that seek to keep you in financial bondage. We've talked about it over and over, but this is a key: God has canceled debt before, and He will cancel yours. But first, you have to ask Him. Then you have to work with Him to bring it into reality.

2. Stop the impulse buys. If you're ever going to be debt free, one basic but often exceedingly difficult step you will have to take is to discipline yourself to stop buying stuff on impulse. Impulse buying is when you see something and immediately decide that you've "got to have it." How many times have you gone to the store without getting what you went there for but still end up leaving with a bunch of other stuff?

The retailers have consumer buying patterns down to such a science that marketing people actually sit in rooms dreaming up ways to strategically display things at checkout counters so that shoppers will feel the urge to buy them. Have you noticed that there never seems to be enough open checkout lanes? Certainly the stores are making enough money to hire a few more checkout clerks. But let me share with you the reason for the closed lanes. The longer people wait in line, the more likely they are to pick up that candy bar or soap opera magazine or, my personal favorite, the incredibly useful Chia Pet gift set. There's a method to the madness—it's to get us to buy more stuff.

I find it impossible to believe that anybody has ever gone to a store planning to buy a Chia Pet! But we do. The marketers are after us, but we need to learn to resist. We have to stop the impulse buys. *Kick the habit.* It won't be easy. Understand that the process is going to be painful. It's going to hurt at first, because if there's anything in life that's difficult to do, it's telling yourself no. It's hard to exercise self-discipline, but it's something we must learn—not just for the sake of saving our money but for saving our souls. In Matthew 16:26, Jesus asks, "For what is a man profited, if he shall gain the whole world, and lose his own soul?" We must learn to deny ourselves before we can live truly satisfying lives. This is both a matter of economic and spiritual discipline.

3. Keep a written budget. Disciplining ourselves financially will require us to get into the habit of writing things down. We must learn to record our total earnings and expenses. What things fall into the "Necessary Purchase" column, and what things are "Extras"? Getting out of debt means that anything that does not fall under "Necessary Purchase" is off-limits. You cannot afford to buy "Extras" until your money becomes yours again because the sad reality is that as long as you're in debt, any money you earn really belongs to your creditors. The goal is to reclaim your money and your financial independence. Keeping a visual log of your spending will help you accomplish this. Some people choose to use computer software programs like Quicken® or Money® to manage their budgets. But all you really need is a notebook, a pencil, and a calculator (if you're like me and have trouble doing math in your head).

At first it may be difficult to muster the discipline and willpower to maintain a family budget. But this is something you'll need to do to keep yourselves accountable to the realities of your finances. It's easy to spend more and more money when you don't have a real-life picture of what your money situation looks like. But if you constantly keep a snapshot of your budget in mind, it will be a little harder to put that extra gallon of ice cream in the shopping cart, or to buy that new CD player for the family room. Your budget tells you that some things will just have to wait.

4. Cut up the credit cards. That's right, you've got to do plastic surgery. Not on your nose or double chin, but on your credit cards. You need to sit down with a pair of sharp scissors and go at it. Chop, chop, chop. Cut 'em up! As painful as it may be, you've got to do it. If you want to get out of debt, you've got to eliminate everything but the essentials, and charge cards are rarely used to pay for the essentials.

Charge cards are without a doubt among the top reasons why people cannot escape the debt trap. The interest rates alone will keep you in bondage for years to come. We intentionally avoid reading the fine print on our billing statements

because we don't want to be reminded of this. Say you're paying the $50 minimum payment on a charge card debt of
$2,000. At a 20 percent annual interest rate, it could take you
more than five years to pay off that debt. You will have paid
more than triple the original amount when you finally fin-
ish the payment. And the credit card people love it! Although
you may have thought how nice of them to be in business just
so they can help you furnish your house or pay for your car
repairs, don't fool yourself; their main reason for being in business is to stay in business. They are delighted at the fact that
you're taking your sweet time in paying them back. That just
means more income for them!

As part of this step, you should also close any open charge
accounts. Everywhere that you have an open charge account
—even if it's the hardware store on the corner—you've got
to close it. If they let you charge stuff, close your account. The
goal is to only use money that you have in your pocket or
bank account to pay for things.

5. Avoid dining out. You might be hungry as you're
walking through the food court at the mall, but can you really afford five dollars for a piece of pizza? Eating out costs a
lot of money. Not only are you paying for the food itself,
you're also paying the long-haired guy who's cooking it and
the bored-looking teenager who is slowly getting around to
finally taking your order. And then there's the lease payment
for the mall space and the TV commercials that advertise the
restaurant's kids' meal deal. Sure, that Big Bacon Double
Mushroom Burger tastes really good—but you do the math.

You need to stick to this plan on a daily basis. Sure, it's easy
to go out to lunch with folks from the office every day, but
have you added up how much money you may be wasting?
Bring your lunch to work. In addition, you should have a

smart plan for your meals at home. For example, don't cook a new dinner until all the leftovers are gone. Learn to take the food that you don't eat, put it into the refrigerator, and eat it the next day. In our nation of plenty, it has become really easy for many of us to throw a perfectly good chicken dinner away without giving it a second thought. Whether it's food or automobiles, we have to get away from the mind-set that causes us to throw good things away to make room for something new and different.

6. Find inexpensive recreational activities. No matter how much debt you have, your family will still need to do things as a family. That may mean a few dollars here and there for a movie rental, gas money to the park, or a date for Mom and Dad. In reality, it doesn't take much money to do things together as a family. In fact, the cheapest activities often turn out to be the most fun.

7. Gang up on bills. One of the ultimate goals of this plan, of course, is to start eliminating your bills. And a strategic way to go at it is to start with the smallest bills first. One of the mistakes we make is that we try to tackle the biggest bills first. We pay on that bill for $11,000—and we pay and pay but never seem to make any headway. Meanwhile, there's a bill over here for $500 that we figure we'll get around to eventually, and it just sits there waiting. It probably annoys us just as much as the $11,000 bill, but we allow it to sit there collecting dust.

It is better to pay off that small bill and get it out of the way. Then the payment that you would pay on that small bill can be applied to the next slightly larger bill, since the smaller bill is gone. Don't take the money you would pay on the smaller bill and say, "Now that bill's gone, I can buy something else." Don't act like you've got some extra money just because one bill is gone. As long as you're in debt, you don't have *extra* money because you're still in debt! Instead, you should take that freed-up money and gang up on the next bill. Take each bill in ascending order until you've eliminated all of them.

8. Pay God first. I saved the most important principle for now. It's later in the list, but you knew it was coming. Before you do anything else, give back to God. You can never get God's help in debt elimination by eliminating God from your plan. You must include God in your debt elimination, and one way to do that is to pay God first.

Remember, Jesus told us to seek first the kingdom. You're worried about clothes and cars and houses and sending your kids to college and all that stuff? Seek first the kingdom of God and then all the rest will be provided for you. In chapter two, we discussed the joy of operating under an open heaven. Well, this is how we begin that process—by giving God His due.

9. Pay yourself (after your debt is gone). Giving back to God is the most crucial principle in this list. But then, after you've given God His tenth, pay yourself. What's wrong with giving yourself a tenth, too? We will never get to the point where we live out of our savings until we have a savings saved. You won't be able to start buying things with cash if you are not storing up cash.

But it must be emphasized: *Don't start saving money until you've paid off all your bills.* Mathematically speaking, saving money while paying off debt works against your money. For example, if you have a Discover Card that charges 21 percent interest and, rather than paying off the bill, you decide you're going to start putting money into a savings account, you're losing money. Why? Because the interest you earn in the savings account will likely be in the 4 percent range, yet you're paying 21 percent interest on what you owe. This means that you are losing 17 percent interest because the interest earned on your savings is far surpassed by the interest you're paying on that bill. If however you are debt free and you do have extra money, bank it or invest it (we'll talk about that in chapter five). Put it to work! Start paying yourself for the future.

10. Celebrate your victories. Every time you pay off a bill, celebrate by praising God and telling somebody about what you've accomplished. Tell them, "I took care of that $40 bill. Now I'm about to wipe out that $150 bill!" Let your small victories help you win bigger victories. Celebrate your progress.

MOVING INTO PRAISE

In the last chapter, we looked at David's victory over Goliath. David was filled with confidence in his God, but do you know what else motivated him? Smaller victories. When King Saul heard that a young shepherd boy was ready to take on Goliath, he was amazed. He told David he was too young to fight the giant, but David responded:

Thy servant kept his father's sheep, and there came a lion, and a bear, and took a lamb out of the flock: And I went out after him, and smote him, and delivered it out of his mouth: and when he arose against me, I . . . slew him. Thy servant slew both the lion and the bear: and this uncircumcised Philistine shall be as one of them, seeing he hath defied . . . the living God. (1 Samuel 17:34–36)

David let his past victories catapult him to his next victory. He knew that if he had done it before, he could do it again.

So, every time you pay off a bill, shout and celebrate and thank God for that victory. And then move on to the next one. That's how the William and Carolyn Jones family did it. At first, their mountain of debt appeared insurmountable. But as they began the program, they saw that it could be done.

First, Carolyn began to pray more seriously about her family's situation. "I had not been asking God to help us get out of debt, mainly because I knew that it was our fault," she says. "But then I started praying and believing that God was going to deliver us." She says prayer changed her family's attitude and empowered them to press on.

Next, she wrote down how much interest her family was paying on each of their bills. She was horrified! She then estimated what they could save if they started paying the debt off quickly rather than spreading it out over several years.

"I'm the kind of person who has to see things to really believe them," Carolyn says. "So when I looked at the numbers on paper, it began to make sense."

Carolyn also began keeping a family budget, complete with detailed earnings and expenses. She was ashamed at how much money the family wasted on unnecessary stuff. "It brought tears to my eyes," she says. "We were making good money, but we weren't saving any of it."

Convicted by the numbers, the Joneses made prompt changes. The charge cards were immediately cut up. Carolyn's shopping sprees were abolished, and her visits to the beauty salon were drastically reduced. The annual family trip to the Wisconsin Dells was postponed indefinitely, and the family started going to the dollar movie theater for entertainment. At the same time, they continued their practice of tithing to the church. They discovered that it became easier to give as they saw more of their money being freed up. They began paying more on their bills, too. Soon William received a promotion, which boosted their money supply even further. Then the Joneses sold their house, making a hefty profit that helped them buy a new home and pay off even more bills.

The little and big areas of savings added up for the Joneses. Consequently, they were able to pay off their $80,000 debt in just one year. (Something to note here is that they did it as a family—husband, wife, and children. Remember, it has to be a family endeavor.)

Today, the Joneses praise God for their financial freedom. They have more money now, but their spending and saving habits continue to be measured and wise. They have made the debt-freedom principles a way of life.

In the next chapters, we will continue to focus on principles for getting out of debt. But we will also focus on *staying* out of debt—and maximizing the new money that you will have as a result.

CHAPTER 4

OUT OF DEBT—PART 2: DISCOVERING TOTAL FREEDOM

OUT OF DEBT—PART 2: DISCOVERING TOTAL FREEDOM

S alem Baptist Church has striven to be used by God in Chicago since we began in 1985. For five years the congregation met in a rented church building on the Near South Side before being transplanted to our Far South Side location.

We purchased our current facility—a brick cathedral and school building—from the Catholic archdiocese in 1990. In addition to church services and outreach ministries to assist the poor and needy, we operate a fully equipped day care, a five hundred-student elementary school, and Chicago's largest Christian bookstore.

My philosophy has always been, "If you're going to dream, you might as well dream big." Consequently, at Salem Baptist Church we've set some very high goals. Of course, we work our way up to the more radical goals. God has taught me that you must first build a church's confidence through small victories and then steadily advance to the big goals. You must use this same strategy as you move toward a debt-free lifestyle.

Sixteen years ago Salem Baptist Church set a goal to have the largest Sunday school in Chicagoland. We started with an average of just fifty people in Sunday school. Today we have two thousand. In 1999, we set a goal to see twenty-five thousand people come to Christ. In order to achieve that goal, the saints of Salem started devoting themselves to prayer and fasting—and nonstop evangelism. What happened? By year's end, we saw almost twenty-seven thousand people profess faith in Jesus Christ. At least four thousand of those have become active members of our church.

When we moved into the community, many residents were wary of our intentions. They worried that we would bring needless noise and traffic. With hundreds of cars parked along the streets on Sundays, it does get crowded. But we went to our neighbors and asked them to be a part of the church. We told them we were there to be a positive, transforming force in the neighborhood. Through time, we earned their trust by putting action behind our message. For instance, we provide jobs. We are currently Roseland's largest employer, with more than 150 on staff.

Down the street from our sanctuary is a three-flat apartment building that once served as a post for neighborhood drug dealers. Salem Baptist Church eventually bought the building and turned it into a fully equipped day care center so that parents would have a safe and reliable place to leave their children during worship services. The residents could see that we were indeed there to be salt and light—to help bring needed change to the 'hood.

I share this information as a way of getting us into the theme of *getting out of debt completely—and staying that way.* Though it's a challenge to plant a church in an economically depressed area like Roseland, God has empowered us to do it. What's more, He has helped us bring both spiritual and economic revitalization to the community. There is much more to be done, but the work has started.

Now, as challenging as it was to bring Salem Baptist Church to Roseland, it is even more of a task to keep it going. It takes faith, perseverance, and a commitment to the good work that God has begun. It's the same with our financial situations. It will be hard to make that initial escape from the bondage of debt. But after you've tasted success, you cannot let your guard down. You will need to reaffirm your desire to be debt free in order to stay in that position. Know that it will take renewed faith, perseverance, and commitment. In a sense, you will have to replay the earlier lessons you've learned over and over.

At Salem, we encourage people to wear regular clothing. Many churches in the African-American community tend to perpetuate the notion that a person has to be all dressed up in order to step into God's house. "If you don't have the fanciest dresses or suits, then don't even bother going up in there," is said about some churches. As a result, they inadvertently reinforce the culture of excess that ensnares many black churchgoers. Of course, there is nothing wrong with looking nice in church. Gathering together to worship and praise the almighty God should be viewed as a special event, but dressing up in the most elaborate fashions is not a prerequisite to be in God's presence. We can worship Him just as effectively in blue jeans and a sweater as we can in an Armani suit.

My wife, Jamell, has taken this message to heart. Typically in African-American churches, the pastor's wife is looked

upon as some type of prominent matriarch and the trend-
setter for fashion among the women of the congregation.
Jamell is in no way a fashion slouch; she is a beautiful, stylish
woman who likes a dazzling ensemble just as much as the next
lady. However, not long after I presented the "Debt Free in
2003" series, she decided she would set a different type of
example for the people of Salem. As a form of fasting, she
decided to refrain from buying new clothes for a year. As a result, others followed her lead. Jamell's example sent a subtle
message to the congregation that this stuff is real. We need
to control our financial destiny—and that will require us to
curb our appetite for material things. It's hard to be faithful to
the debt-free lifestyle when there's overwhelming social pressure in our churches that often seduces us to project an image
that is above our means.

Your freedom is a gift from God, but it is also a responsi-
bility. You will be responsible for managing your money in a
way that will sustain your financial freedom and also bring
blessings to others. You will have to become adept at running your life with an ongoing awareness of the pitfalls and
dangers of money. And it won't be easy.

One of the hardest things to do, it seems, is to keep our
own lives running in proper order. That may be why it's so
easy for us to run other people's lives. Have you noticed that?
It's very easy to judge other people: "Why is she wearing
that?" "Why does he talk like that?" We always think we
know what's best for other folks. That's just the way we are,
because God has programmed each one of us to run a life. We
are wired that way. We're not happy if we don't have a life to
run. But the truth is that the life He programmed us to run
is not someone else's but our own. Yours is the only life that
you have jurisdiction over. Although it's infinitely easier to
impose our opinions on somebody else's life rather than run

our own, if we're going to keep on track with a debt-free lifestyle, we must make sure we concentrate all of our efforts on running our own lives.

WE ARE HOUSES DIVIDED

And if a kingdom be divided against itself, that kingdom cannot stand. And if a house be divided against itself, that house cannot stand." (Mark 3:24–25)

Let's talk specifically about becoming totally debt free. If you put into action the principles set forth in this chapter, you can be completely out of debt in five years.

In the last chapter, when I spoke of getting out of debt, it pertained to everything except the mortgage, car note, insurance, and utilities. In this chapter, when I speak of getting out of debt, I'm talking about *out of debt*. That means your credit cards, your doctor bills, your car, and even your house. (The insurance and utility bills will always be with us, so for our purposes here, let's remove them from the category of "debt.")

If we are going to get out of debt, we might as well go all the way. Get rid of those credit cards. Get rid of that pesky car note. Get rid of that high mortgage payment. These are realistic and achievable goals. (I should note, however, that while paying off a mortgage early is a wise move for most people, it might not be the best move for everybody. If your mortgage rates are low, and if the tax-deductible mortgage interest from a home loan reduces your tax burden by a significant enough amount, then from an economic perspective you may be better off keeping your mortgage. But that is probably not the case for most folks. Still, it's a good idea to consider your overall financial picture carefully and consult with a tax planner before deciding to go all the way in paying off your house.)

Remember, he whom the Son sets free is free indeed (see John 8:36). Therefore, you don't have to leave any area behind. Depending on how much you owe on your house, you can be free from all of your debts in as little as five years. (If your mortgage is higher than average, it may take up to seven years.)

In Mark 3, Jesus said that a house divided against itself cannot stand. As an African-American pastor, I'm always excited about what God allows us to do within the parameters of the church. As a by-product of segregation in America, many social structures and information sources common to the rest of society were not made available to the black community. As a result, we have historically had to use the church for everything. We've used the church to discuss parenting and child rearing. We've used the church to learn about our history. We've used the church as a rallying point for political action. We've even used the church as a place to learn about financial issues. Though the African-American community has had to deal with these issues in the church setting by necessity, in many ways it is an appropriate thing, particularly since money really is a spiritual matter. American churches in general would do well to teach their congregants about the spiritual aspects of money and financial planning.

Most Americans want the same things out of life. We all would like to one day own our own home. We all would like to be able to put some money in the bank for the future. We all would like to be able to send our children to college and have enough money left over to enjoy a comfortable retirement. We set out to do that by paying our bills on a monthly basis, thinking that at some point our dreams will come true. Sadly, though, if you pay your bills at the rate you are paying them now and think that the debt-free life is right around the corner, you are the living embodiment of what I call "a house divided against itself."

Let me say that for you another way. If you pay your bills the way you're paying them now, month by month, and think that the debt-free life is an achievable goal, think again. You are a house divided against itself. Why? Because your mind is thinking one way while your actions are taking you in a different direction. You may be earnestly determined to get out of debt someday, but reality is holding you back. Your actions—that is, paying your bills month by month—are taking you in the opposite direction. And, as a result, you become a house divided against itself.

Why? Because no matter how faithful you are to the bill-paying program, you cannot make any truly noteworthy progress paying down your bills in this way.

The following sentence may sound cynical to some people, but it's true: The American financial system is set up so that people in debt will always be in debt. That's the way of the world. That's the name of the game. In a sort of ironic and perverse way, keeping people in debt drives our financial system. So, if you're not careful, you will find yourself in a hole. Even if you pay your bills on time each month, you will still fall short of breaking even, and you can definitely abandon any hope of ever getting ahead.

We strive all of our lives to get an A#1 credit rating. No one wants a tarnished credit record. But the reason we want an unblemished credit rating is so that when we see something we really want, we can just go out and get it. Therefore on that basis we look at an A#1 credit rating as a wonderful blessing. But it's not a wonderful blessing. While I morally urge you to make sure that you pay those who you owe, understand that your A#1 credit rating is not a plus for you; it's a plus for the credit card companies, but not for you.

If given the option, it is better to be able to buy whatever you want with cash than to use credit. Buying stuff outright with our own money should be our greatest economic ambition. However, we carry around the notion that we will never be able to buy things flat out with our own cash. So, consequently, we rejoice when we see that our credit rating is A#1. We praise God when we discover that Visa and MasterCard have upped our spending limit. That means we're in the game—we've got access to wealth. But it's not *our* wealth. The wealth belongs to the bank and the credit card company. Nevertheless, we feel privileged that they would give us the opportunity to use their money. We've got it all backwards.

Think about it: Credit card companies, mortgage companies, and automobile financing companies are among the richest institutions in America, and they have no conscious plan or desire to see people become debt free. The plan of the lender is to keep the borrower paying as long as he possibly can. With interest rates added on to the loans and long-term payment plans in place, in the end it always means more money for the lender and less for the borrower. So the borrower never gets ahead. No one is against your having a good credit rating. The financial institutions want you to have A#1 credit. They encourage it. That is why you get credit cards in the mail for which you never applied. Your good credit rating ensures that eventually there will be an opportunity for more money in the bank for the lenders. But what about your bank account? Who's putting money in there?

Have you ever seriously contemplated just how much money we're giving away to banks and mortgage companies? Before I presented this message to my church, I sat down and calculated how much money my congregation might be spending on mortgage payments. I looked at the then ten thousand-member roll, estimated the number of households, and figured that at least half of them were buying a house. At that rate, the members of Salem Baptist Church were probably paying at least $1 billion on home mortgages. Many people in my congregation were shocked by this astounding figure. We are giving away truckloads of money to banks and mortgage companies. I asked my parishioners, "Could you imagine the church we could build or the needy people we could feed and employ with $1 billion?" They were speechless. I said, "Do you know how much monetary strength we could inject into the Roseland economy? We could attract reputable businesses and renovate entire neighborhoods."

The whole concept of debt, and our conventional way of paying it off, is designed to keep us poor and make others rich. It is the way of the world. For example, if you buy a house for $250,000 and pay $50,000 down, you are most likely financing $200,000 over a period of thirty years. By the time it is all said and done, when you add the finance charges you will pay on that $200,000, you have actually paid back $600,000! You have paid your $200,000 back plus the mortgage company profits at a 200 percent level! In other words, you literally have just given away $400,000. Did you ever stop to think that if you make $40,000 a year, you will have to work an extra ten years just to pay off the interest? In reality you would have to work longer than that because the ten years, of course, assumes that every dime of your check goes toward that interest payment.

Think of it another way: If you buy a house when your child is a five-year-old in kindergarten, you will have to work until your child is a sophomore in high school just to pay off the interest on your mortgage. Ouch! That's ten winters of getting up at 5 A.M. and your car not starting. That's ten years of morning and evening rush hours on a jam-packed highway. That's ten years of typing, dictating, selling, bean counting—or whatever your job happens to be. That's ten whole years of your life spent working to give somebody else extra money. Doesn't that seem like a lot of wasted effort? Doesn't that strike you as a massive waste of money? You are working to get ahead, but the energy you are expending, in some ways, is futile.

It does not end with mortgages. Consider a Visa or a department store charge card with a 19 percent interest rate. In reality, you're going to pay one and a half times the original amount of whatever it is that you purchased with that card—probably, by the way, something for which you could have waited, or even more likely, done without.

I cannot say it enough: Mortgages, auto loans, and credit cards are the sources of the most serious financial problems facing most Americans. Most of us owe somebody something. Debt has become a strong man that is holding us captive. We can't do what we want to do as a church, we can't do what we want to do as a community, we can't do what we want to do as families because debt is holding us captive. Just think about all the stuff you could do if you didn't owe anything. Just think about how much of an offering you could give to your church and to charitable organizations if you didn't owe anything to anybody.

BIND THE STRONG MAN

And if Satan rise up against himself, and be divided, he cannot stand, but hath an end. No man can enter a strong man's house, and spoil his goods, except he first bind the strong man; and then he will spoil his house. (Mark 3:26–27)

Debt has become a strong man who is keeping us from being financially free. Jesus said that you cannot enter a strong man's house and spoil his goods unless you first bind the strong man. The truth is that debt is a strong man who has invaded *our* houses. He has set up camp there, and he's living the good life. He has taken over, and he's having his way with us. If we're going to get rid of him, we've got to bind him.

The strong man must be restrained before you can regain control of your life. You've got to get that strong man out of your house. In order to do that, you must first find a way to bind him. Before we address that pressing matter, let me first reiterate a couple of important facts and chart the course of where we will be going in the remainder of this book. First of all, *we will never get ahead by paying off our bills on a monthly basis only*. This is a lie that America has sold us, and we've bought it. We think that if we just keep paying and paying each month that we are eventually going to get ahead. Not true. You will never get ahead that way.

Second, *it is wrong to give the mortgage company two to three times more money than you really have to*. If you're paying an extra $400,000 in interest on a $200,000 mortgage, then you're wasting a lot of money and effort. The mortgage company does not want you to know that there is another way.

Third, by changing your mind and your behavior *you can actually pay off all your bills in about five years* and be totally debt free. This is an achievable goal.

Fourth, after you pay off your bills, *you can take the money you were giving away to the mortgage company and the credit card company, invest it wisely, and live for the rest of your life almost entirely off the interest* earned on the money that you used to give away. This, too, is a doable goal.

At this point, you might wonder, "So what's the problem, Preacher? If it is that simple, why is it that the majority of church people are sitting around in debt? And why is it that we don't know that we can get out of it?" I'm glad you asked. Look at what the apostle Paul told the saints in Corinth:

For we know in part, and we prophesy in part. But when that which is perfect is come, then that which is in part shall be done away. When I was a child, I spake as a child, I understood as a child, I thought as a child: but when I became a man, I put away childish things. For now we see through a glass, darkly; but then face to face: now I know in part; but then shall I know even as also I am known. (1 Corinthians 13:9–12)

Allow me to adapt Paul's excellent metaphor for our purposes here. At this point in time, we are looking at our financial situation as if through a "glass darkly," and we think that debt is something that everybody has and that everybody is going to always have. I contend that the reason we are in debt is that we cannot see the big picture. We cannot see this thing clearly. We only know a fraction of the story. God said that people and nations are destroyed because of a lack of knowledge (Hosea 4:6). We're lacking knowledge because we have not seen clearly. We have only known in part. But now is the time for us to grow up and see the big picture and learn the full story.

As Paul said, "When I was a child, I spake as a child, I understood as a child, I thought as a child: but when I became a man, I put away childish things." My friend, it is childish behavior to desire or to buy everything you see and to not take control of your financial destiny. Children do that kind of stuff. They have no regard for how much stuff costs, nor do they care. All they know is that it's a new Koby Bryant shoe or a new Sony PlayStation. Children see stuff and they start to drool. They've got to have it—now! As adults, we have to get it through our heads: When we were children, it was understandable that we acted like that. But there comes a time, my fellow adult, when we must become spiritually—and financially

—mature. Somebody is going to have to say it's time for us to "grow up" and stop giving all of our money to the credit card company and to the mortgage company. It is time for us to take control of our own financial destiny. If you are not able to do that, it is because you are financially (and very likely spiritually) childish.

One of the dictionary definitions of adulthood is "maturity, the ability to know what is best and then to sacrifice on the behalf of what is best." Do you know what's best for your financial destiny? It is possible for you to be debt free in five years. But in order for you to do that, you've got to come up with a new strategy and sacrifice on behalf of that strategy. You cannot continue to pay your bills month by month with no regard for your financial future. You need a new strategy. Otherwise, you are operating in immaturity.

THE FIVE-YEAR PLAN

Look at Table 4.1, "Salem Baptist Church Five-Year Debt-Free Program" at the end of this chapter. While I recognize that every reader's financial profile may be different, let's look at Joe and Mary Member as models of the average American family. They might have some bills you do not have, or a lower mortgage payment, but pay that no mind. For now, Joe and Mary will represent the average American family. This chart contains the basic formula that we will use to move toward becoming totally debt free.

In the first column of the chart, you will see the various debts of Mr. and Mrs. Member. The column next to it shows their current balances on each of the debts. They owe $445 on their Discover Card. They still owe $9,200 on their car loan. They took out a home equity loan. They owe Visa $1,025 and MasterCard $1,892. And then there is the mortgage, on which they still owe $72,000. I realize that your mortgage is probably more than that, but work with me here.

The next column shows Joe and Mary's current monthly payment schedule. They are currently paying Discover $20, the minimum amount due—exactly the way Discover likes it. The monthly car loan payment is $303. The monthly mortgage payment is $890, and on and on. In aggregate, Joe and Mary's debt totals $89,562. They have nearly $90,000 worth of debt, and they want to get out from under it. Their monthly payments total $1,448 per month. But look at the annual rate of interest on their various bills. These are actual figures, by the way. That Discover Card you may have in your wallet right now is charging you 19.8 percent interest on your balance. The average car note is at 13.8 percent; average home equity loan at 9.6 percent; and the average mortgage at 8.24 percent. That Visa card you have is charging you an annual rate of 16.5 percent, and your MasterCard is charging you an annual rate of 21 percent.

Now watch what happens when Joe and Mary continue to pay their bills at the current monthly rate. It will take them two years to pay off Discover; three years to pay off the car, the home equity loan, and Visa; three and a half years to pay off MasterCard; and the big one—thirty years to pay off the house note. But there's more. The next column reveals the total amount that Joe and Mary will be paying including interest at their present pace. Once you factor in the interest, they will pay $272,491. Back in the balance column, we can see that they only borrowed $89,562. But, when all is said and done, they will have paid back $272,491. That's more than three times the amount they borrowed! Just think about all the extra money that Joe and Mary are giving away for the privilege of borrowing other people's money.

But there's hope for Joe and Mary Member. If they were

to follow the plan that we have laid out in this book, and pay off their debts early, they can save $151,408. Who could be against that? They can save money! If Joe and Mary follow their conventional bill payment method, then thirty years from now, they would have given away an extra $151,000—and that's just on a mortgage of $72,000. Those of us with $200,000 mortgages will be giving away loads more.

But how can Joe and Mary Member erase that kind of debt in five years? Let's look. If they were able to come up with an extra $250 beyond what they are paying now on monthly bills, amazing things could happen. (You might ask, "Where would the $250 extra come from?" Well, Joe and Mary would have to go back to the last chapter and read about the "Ten Steps to Debt Freedom." The bottom line is this: There are plenty of areas where money can be "found" once we stop spending it in a wasteful manner.)

Look at the formula on the chart. If Joe and Mary Member add that extra $250 to the monthly payment of their first bill, the Discover Card, that would mean they'd be paying $270 a month toward that debt. At that rate, Joe and Mary will pay off that first bill in just two months. Once that bill is paid in full, they can take the same $250—plus the $20 from the first bill—and add it to what they are paying on their car note. That would give them a total of $573 for their car payment. At that rate, they will pay off the car note in sixteen months rather than three years. Once that bill is paid in full, Joe and Mary can take the same $250, plus the $20, plus the $303 that would have gone towards their car payment, and apply it all to the home equity loan. Now they have $733 for their home equity payment. They will pay that one off in four months. Guess what happens when that bill is paid off? You're absolutely right, once the home equity loan is paid off they can take the original $250, plus the $20, plus the $303, plus the $160 from the home equity loan, plus the $30 Visa payment, and in only one month they will have paid off that Visa bill! Once that's paid, they can take all of the money that they have been paying on all the other bills, plus the $45 MasterCard payment—that's $808—and use it to pay off the MasterCard account. At that point, it will only take them two months. Now, with all the other bills gone, all they have left to tackle is the mortgage. If they take all the money they would have been paying on their other bills and add it to the $890 mortgage payment, they will have $1,698. With that amount, it will take Joe and Mary Member three and a half years to pay off their thirty-year mortgage. At the end of the three and a half years, Joe and Mary are officially debt free. Whew!

When it's over, not only are Joe and Mary Member debt free, they also have saved $151,000. Instead of giving that money away, they can keep it to work toward their own needs. Just like Joe and Mary, you probably are preparing to give that kind of money away to the banks and mortgage lenders. But let's be realistic about this thing—you don't have money like that to waste. How can you give money of that magnitude away and feel that you are actually "getting ahead"? In order to get ahead, you need to have control over every dime that comes to you.

Before we move forward, let's be clear on one thing. While Joe and Mary Member (i.e., *you*) are targeting a particular bill, they must keep paying the regular payment on the other bills that they've yet to get to. They should not stop and say, "Well, we just won't pay anything on that one until we get finished with this current bill." No, no, no. They still must continue to pay every remaining bill, month by month, just as if nothing has changed. The time will come to double up their efforts on those remaining bills.

Now, watch this. In three and a half years, when Joe and Mary Member's mortgage is paid off, they will have $1,698 that they were paying on the mortgage. But with the mortgage gone, they can now use that money on something that will pay them back—namely, investments. We'll learn more about aggressive investing in the next chapter, but for now let's consider this: If Joe and Mary were to take that $1,698 and invest it monthly in something that will pay them 10 percent on their money over twenty years, in two decades they could have $500,000 in the bank. Don't think that $1,698 is too much money to be putting into investments each month. Remember, if the Members had not paid their mortgage and other bills off early, they would still be paying out that money each month to the banks and the mortgage company—money they would never see again. But instead, twenty years from now, rather than owing money on their house, Joe and Mary will have $500,000. What's more, they can then take that $500,000 and invest it in a low-risk vehicle with a 10 percent annualized return, and they are able to earn at least $50,000 a year in interest. Remember Elisha's advice to the widow in chapter one?

Whether the numbers are high or low, the goal is to arrive at a point where somebody is paying you for *your* money—not the other way around. Like Joe and Mary Member, you could potentially earn $50,000 a year on your own money. At that rate, you would never need to touch the principal—you can live off of the interest for years to come. You could retire earlier than you had planned, put your kids through college, and pump money into the work of the church and other worthy causes.

We have been sucked in by the American financial system that says we should take our time and pay off our bills on a monthly basis and take thirty years to pay off a mortgage. As a result, we're just giving away extra money that we could be using! That's wrong. It is not the way it ought to be. If we are going to take control of our own financial destiny, we will need to make some hard choices. But if we are faithful and patient in making those initial hard choices, we can lay the foundation for a future that is full of promise and reward.

NEW WINESKINS

Since presenting this five-year formula to my congregation, I've seen incredible things occur. Take, for instance, the experience of a woman we'll call Jane Henry. A thirty-something single mother of two, Jane had been a member of Salem Baptist Church for three years when she heard the "Debt Free in 2003" message. Jane carried a backbreaking load of debt: student loans, car note, credit cards.

As an administrative assistant at a medical office, Jane made a livable wage, but with two kids to feed and clothe, she often felt the strain of making ends meet. Some months, payments were missed and the charge cards became an easy way to buy things after the paycheck was used up. "I had a Visa. I had a Lerner's card. I had a Carson Pirie Scott's card," she recalls. "I just ran them up without even thinking about the possibility that it was going to hurt me later."

But soon, she found herself over the limit. And when she tried to get other cards, her applications were declined. Her credit history, it turns out, was in shambles. "It should not have been a surprise to me," she says, "but I was hurt. When I saw how bad my credit report had become, I cried."

Like anybody else, Jane had her version of the American Dream. She wanted to have enough money to raise her kids properly, and someday she wanted to buy a house. But her financial future looked bleak. She was $10,000 in debt—not to mention food, utilities, and other things that had to be paid for each month. At times she wanted to give up hope, but she prayed that God would help her to help herself out of the financial mess she'd created. When she discovered that we would be discussing principles for getting out of debt, she was elated.

"I hung on every word you said," she told me later. "The Bible says that faith comes by hearing, and my faith was truly restored by hearing those messages." Following each service, she obtained a cassette tape of the sermon. "I played those tapes over and over and over until they nearly broke. I needed to hear that message."

But Jane was not just a hearer of the word; she immediately set out to put the principles into action. She discovered she was able to find extra money in her budget when she stopped spending money on unnecessary things like fast food. She took that extra cash to attack her bills, smallest to largest. "I started paying off the credit card bills," she says. "Then I paid the student loans. Then my car."

Jane started the plan in May of 1998. By May of 1999, all of her debt was gone. Today, she is a debt-free woman who has a new spring in her step. What's more, she recently received word that she'd been approved to buy a house. Nowadays, she is a woman overflowing with praise and thanks to God: "I'm free! I'm free from bondage," she says through tears of joy. "And once you experience this new life and power of Christ's freedom, you don't want to go back to that old lifestyle."

No man putteth a piece of new cloth unto an old garment, for that which is put in to fill it up taketh from the garment, and the rent is made worse. Neither do men put new wine into old bottles: else the bottles break, and the wine runneth out, and

the bottles perish: but they put new wine into new bottles, and
both are preserved. (Matthew 9:16–17)

Most people would never go to a "getting out of debt"
seminar. Most people don't trust the presenters at those kinds
of seminars because we think they're running some sort of
scam. They're just trying to sell us something. Like those sleazy
looking guys in TV infomercials, they just want our money.
But rest assured, I'm not trying to scam you out of your money.
I'm not trying to take you for a ride with the counsel in this
book. Rather, I am trying to empower God's people to maximize their resources so that they can make better use of the
money that they've earned. The bottom line is this: Five years
from now, you can be totally debt free. Five years from now,
you can be putting your money into investments that will pay
you back. Five years from now, you can be putting more money
into the work of your church, into Christian missions, into
outreach to the poor and hungry. The sky is the limit on
how God might lead you to use that extra money. But first
you've got to stop wasting it. Your mind has to change. The
old ways of thinking must be abandoned. You need to become
a new receptacle of God's message of debt deliverance.

Like Jesus said, you don't put an unshrunk cloth on an
old garment—it won't stick. Nor would you put new wine
into old wineskins—the old skins would not be able to handle the potency of that fresh wine. Rather, you need to make
sure the wineskins can handle that new drink. You need new
wineskins—a new container.

If after receiving the message in this book you come to
believe that you can truly become debt free in the next five,
six, or seven years, then you are in possession of new wine.
The power of that belief is like new wine. You have potent
new knowledge—a radical new way of thinking. You can't

take this new wine and put it in old wineskins. In other words, you can't take this new attitude and pay off your bills the same old way. You can't take your new attitude and use your money in the same old ways. It's easy for you to say, "I'm going to be debt free!" But in order to do it, you've got to take this new attitude and new knowledge and put it in a new container. You've got to have a new formula. Paying off your bills while not making new ones is a new formula. Ganging up on your debt is a new formula. You must allow this new attitude about your finances to be lived out in new actions. To paraphrase Paul, we must allow our actions to be transformed by this renewing of our minds (Romans 12:2).

BINDING YOUR OWN BUSINESS

Let's return to the message we explored earlier in Mark 3:27, where the Master offers some helpful principles about how to handle our personal business. The strong man has invaded our homes. He has taken over. But if we want to regain control of our homes and our lives, we've got to bind that strong man. If a kingdom is divided against itself, that kingdom can't stand. A house divided against itself cannot stand. We must bind the strong man. If there's someone in the room with you, tell them: "You must bind the strong man!" If you're alone, say it to yourself: "I must bind the strong man!"

In the gospel of Matthew, Jesus gives us some additional news about this business of "binding."

And I will give unto thee the keys of the kingdom of heaven: and whatsoever thou shalt bind on earth will be bound in heaven; and whatsoever thou shalt loose on earth shall be loosed in heaven. (Matthew 16:19)

Here, Jesus is speaking to Peter regarding the authority that He would soon grant to His church on earth. Jesus indicates that whatever we bind on earth shall be bound in heaven, and whatever we loose on earth shall be loosed in heaven. Today, many Christians go around facetiously binding stuff they can't see: They "bind" this and they "bind" that in the name of Jesus. But what about the binding of debt? Far from some phantom threat to our spiritual well-being, debt is a very real economic and spiritual issue that must be dealt with before we can lead truly productive lives.

The good news is this: Whatever we bind on earth will also be bound in heaven. In other words, if you come up with a plan on earth in order to get yourself financially free and you believe that God can make it happen, He says, "I will help you." Heaven will back you up. Heaven will be on your side. Heaven will be with you. Heaven will stand firm for you. Heaven will stand behind the formula you're using. But before that happens, you've got to come up with something on earth.

When it comes to financial indebtedness, many of God's people are being bound instead of binding. I suspect many of our prayers might sound like this: "O Lord, You've got to help me with these bills. Lord Jesus, I don't know how I got myself into this. I don't know how I let them talk me into signing up to buy this car. I don't know if we can really afford to keep paying for this house. God, I have all this pressure on me. My back is against the wall. Please help me, Lord." But God's response to your situation may not be quite what you're hoping for. Sure, there are examples of instantaneous miracles, where an unexpected check arrives in the mail or a relative leaves you lots of money. But more likely than not, God will probably respond to your desperate prayer with something like this: "You want My help? Fine. Get up off your knees and bind something. Come up with a plan. Come up with a formula to bind that debt, and whatever you bind on earth, I'll help you in heaven. I'll back you up. But if you don't bind anything on earth, I won't have anything to back you up with, because you're not doing anything to help the situation."

We must be doers of the Word and not just hearers, said James. And that's a good principle to carry with us as we approach this matter of becoming debt free. God is ready to lead us out of our indebtedness, but we need to be willing to put ourselves in a position for Him to help us. Let's not just *think* about getting out of debt in five years; let's bind the strong man and begin to *do* it.

Base Margin: $250.00

Table 4.1
Salem Baptist Church Five-Year Debt-Free Program
Financial Plan For
Joseph and Mary Member
July 1998 to December 2003

Debt Name	Balance	Monthly Payment	Annual Rate	Time to Pay Bills at Monthly Payment	Amount Paid with Payment & Interest	Total Savings When Paid Early	Payoff Date
Discover	$445.00	$20.00	19.80%	2 years	$621.00	$176.00	July 1998
Visa	1,025.00	30.00	16.50%	3 years	1,532.00	338.00	May 2000
MasterCard	1,892.00	45.00	21.00%	$3\frac{1}{2}$ years	3,083.00	794.00	July 2000
Car	9,200.00	303.00	13.80%	3 years	10,706.00	1,004.00	Dec. 1999
Home Equity Loan	5,000.00	160.00	9.60%	3 years	6,559.00	1,106.00	April 2000
Mortgage	72,000.00	890.00	8.24%	30 years	249,990.00	147,990.00	Dec. 2003
Total	$89,562.00	$1,448.00			$272,491.00	$151,408.00	

Principal Formula:

Add: $250.00 to your first bill to be paid off

$250.00 +20.00 Discover payment = $270.00 for your Discover card payment — paid off in 2 months

Once that bill is paid in full

$250.00 + 20 from the first bill paid + 303.00 car payment = $573.00 for your car payment — paid off in 16 months

Once that bill is paid in full

$250.00 + 20 + 303 + 160.00 home equity payment = $733.00 for your home equity payment — paid off in 4 months

Once that bill is paid in full

$250.00 + 20 + 303 + 160 + 30.00 Visa payment = $763.00 for your Visa payment — paid off in 1 month

Once that bill is paid in full

$250.00 + 20 + 303 + 160 + 30 + 45.00 MasterCard payment = $808.00 for your MasterCard payment — paid off in 2 months

Once that bill is paid in full

$250.00 + 20 + 303 + 160+ 30 + 45 + 890.00 mortgage payment = $1,698.00 for your mortgage payment — paid off in $3\frac{1}{2}$ years

YOU ARE NOW DEBT FREE IN 2003!

Please note that while you are paying off a bill completely, all other bills must be paid as well.

Example: While paying off your Discover bill, you must continue to make your monthly payments on all other bills.

Discover:	$20.00 + 250.00 = $270.00
Visa:	30.00
MasterCard:	45.00
Car:	303.00
Home Equity:	160.00
Mortgage:	890.00

After your mortgage is paid off you now have $1,698.00 to invest a month + 10% interest over 20 years = $500,000. Invest this $500,000 in Mutual Funds at 10% per year and enjoy $50,000.00 year retirement income without ever touching the principal.

OUT OF IDLENESS: USE IT OR LOSE IT

OUT OF IDLENESS: USE IT OR LOSE IT

*F*or the kingdom of heaven is as a man travelling into a
far country, who called his own servants, and delivered
unto them his goods. And unto one he gave five talents, to another two, and to another one, to every man according to his several ability; and straightway took his journey.
Then he that had received the five talents went and traded
with the same, and made them other five talents. And likewise
he that had received two, he also gained other two. But he that
had received one went and digged in the earth, and hid his
lord's money. After a long time the lord of those servants
cometh, and reckoneth with them. And so he that had received
five talents came and brought other five talents, saying, Lord,
thou deliveredst unto me five talents: behold, I have gained be-
side them five talents more. His lord said unto him, Well done,

thou good and faithful servant: thou hast been faithful over a few things, I will make thee ruler over many things: enter thou into the joy of thy lord. He also that had received two talents came and said, Lord, thou deliveredst unto me two talents: behold, I have gained two other talents besides them. His lord said unto him, Well done, good and faithful servant; thou hast been faithful over a few things, I will make thee ruler over many things: enter thou into the joy of thy lord. Then he which had received the one talent came and said, Lord, I knew thee that thou art an hard man, reaping where thou hast not sown, and gathering where thou hast not strawed. And I was afraid, and went and hid thy talent in the earth: lo, there thou hast that is thine. His lord answered and said unto him, Thou wicked and slothful servant, thou knewest that I reap where I sowed not, and gather where I have not strawed. Thou oughtest therefore to have put my money to the exchangers, and then at my coming I should have received mine own with usury. Take therefore the talent from him, and give it unto him which hath ten talents. For unto every one that hath shall be given, and he shall have abundance: but from him that hath not shall be taken away even that which he hath. And cast ye the unprofitable servant into outer darkness: there shall be weeping and gnashing of teeth. (Matthew 25:14–30)

There's an easy way to summarize Jesus' point in this parable of the talents: You either use it or you lose it. It's as simple as that. You either put what you've been given into use or, one way or the other, it will be taken from you.

I believe that we need to be constantly reminded of the importance of using what we have. As human creatures, it becomes very easy to take our resources and abilities for granted. A popular urban legend that made its way into many a pastor's sermon before it began to be questioned observes that human beings only use 10 percent of their brain's total capacity. The implication is that we have barely tapped into our full potential intellectually. Though scientists have exposed the falsity of that claim, there is definitely truth to the idea that as men and women created in the image of God, we seldom approach the zenith of our true potential. Could you imagine all the things we could be doing if we used our whole head and heart? Paul's tried but true claim—"I can do all things through Christ"—is not just a boast of God's power, but also a challenge for us to pursue greatness in His name.

Failure to use what we have most often results in losing what we have. If you tied your arms to your body and didn't use them for two months, when you finally tried to use them again it's possible that they would not respond. It's possible that gangrene would have set in and that your arms would need to be amputated. Whatever you don't use, you lose.

If you have the ability to play the piano but don't play for ten years, when you sit back down at the keyboard that ability won't be there for you the way it once was. If you have the ability to teach and don't do it for ten years, when you finally stand up before a class again it will take you a long time to get back into that role. It's the same no matter what endeavor you pursue: basketball, crocheting, cooking, driving a car. It doesn't matter. If you have a skill and don't put it to use, that skill will deteriorate over time—and possibly be lost for good. Use it or lose it.

In Matthew 24 and 25, Jesus was trying to drive home a point to His disciples about the importance of stewardship—that is, the importance of maximizing your time and abilities for God while you still have time and abilities. As Jesus sat on the Mount of Olives, His disciples came to Him seeking information about the end of the world and the coming of His kingdom. Jesus volunteers some of the juicy End Times signs they should watch out for, but then He unleashes a series of parables dealing with the overwhelming importance of faithfulness and stewardship. His concluding parable is the story of the talents. A rich man is about to take a long trip, but before he departs he summons his three servants and gives them each a certain number of talents. The number each man receives is based on his individual ability: the first servant gets five, the second gets two, and the other receives just one. In Jesus' day, a talent referred to a large sum of money equal to about two years' wages. However, based on the universal lesson of the parable, many have taken the word *talent* to signify one's natural gifts and acquired skills.

And so the rich man leaves the servants to do what they will with their master's money. Clearly, the rich man had more than a passing understanding of his servants' abilities, for he did not give them equal amounts (as in Luke's account of a similar parable of Jesus in Luke 19). Rather, he gave them money proportionate to what he perceived their skills and tendencies to be. The man with the largest sum of talents went and traded—i.e., invested—the money and doubled his amount. The man with the second largest sum of talents traded his money, too, and doubled that investment. Ah, but the man with just one talent went and hid his master's money in the ground.

When the rich man returned to town, he wanted to know how his money had been put to use. The servant who was given five talents showed his master that he had doubled that amount. The servant who had been given two talents also showed his master a twofold increase. Both of these men were rewarded, it appears, with riches and authority. Ah, but the servant who had been given one talent . . .

It should not go unnoticed that this parable is in many ways typical of everyday life. One of the most telling parallels is that the guy who did the least was also the one who talked the most. The servant who had been entrusted with one talent said, "Master, you're a tough businessman, doing this and that. And I knew you'd come back asking me all kinds of questions, but my mama got sick and my baby ran out of formula and my lady didn't have any Pampers for him. It's just been a hectic time for us. Anyway, I was afraid and running short on time. So I buried your money. Here it is, just like you left it." The last servant came up with all of these excuses for why he didn't do anything with the money.

But the rich man was unsympathetic. He told the servant, "You wicked and lazy bum! At least you could have put my money in a savings account, where it could have earned a little bit of interest." He then took the talent from the lazy servant and gave it to the servant who had earned him the most money.

Jesus makes a key point here about our faithfulness: Everyone who has something will be given even more—because he knows what to do with it. But the guy who has nothing will be stripped of the little he has—because he does not use what he has been given. In other words, use it or lose it.

ON EARTH AS IT IS IN HEAVEN

When I was a growing up in the church, I heard this parable regularly. Back then when we would discuss this passage, we usually focused on the idea of spiritual service. We'd say, "If you don't use the talent that the Lord has given you, you will lose it." And so we would talk about singing, preaching, teaching, working with youth, and so on. A Christian is expected to exercise his or her talents. In the kingdom of God, the Lord gives us something to do, and if we don't do it then what we've been given can be lost.

That's true, but I've also come to believe that this piece of Scripture is one of the greatest biblical teachings on the proper use of money—and it comes directly from the lips of Jesus. This passage seems to clearly suggest that God wants us to invest the money He gives us, and if we don't use it wisely, we will lose it.

When the rich man says, "Well done, thou good and faithful servant; . . . I will make thee ruler over many things," we tend to think that passage refers only to our arrival in heaven. I grew up hearing the deacon saying, "I just want to hear the Lord say, 'Well done!'" We used to reserve that notion just for heaven. But you know what? When I look at my bank account, I want to hear Him say, "Well done!" Don't get me wrong; we still should look forward to hearing those words when we arrive in heaven. However, we also should long to hear and feel those words while we're here on earth. And when I look at my financial life, I want to know in my heart that God is pleased with how I've been handling the little bit He has given me.

My friend, if we don't invest the money we have, we will lose it. God is concerned about what we do with our money. The Bible says that every good and perfect gift is from above. Money, when kept in proper perspective, is a good and helpful thing. So that means that God gives it to us. And He is concerned about what we do with it.

Now, think about it like this: Everyone who knows what to do with money can get more of it. If you want more money, do the right thing with the little bit that you have. If you do the right thing with the little bit that you have, you will always be able to get some more. But if you don't do what's right with the little bit . . . We have a spiritual obligation to maximize the gifts God has entrusted to us.

MONEY MATTERS

"He that is faithful in that which is least is faithful also in much: and he that is unjust in the least is unjust also in much." (Luke 16:10)

Did you know that the Bible contains seven hundred direct references to money? Two-thirds of the parables of Jesus and one out of every six New Testament verses deal with the right and wrong use of material possessions. Yet Christians rarely talk in a church setting about things like investing their money.

Many Christians consider it unspiritual to talk about investing in this life. They think focusing on increasing earthly wealth is synonymous with being materialistic and failing to trust God. Certainly putting all of your life's eggs into this one basket is not a wise thing, but if you fool around and do not invest your money in anything and the Lord tarries and you don't die, you're going to find yourself in a position where you must depend on somebody else to take care of you.

Investing your money is not an unspiritual thing. Because Jesus says, "Lay not up for yourselves treasures upon earth, where moth and rust doth corrupt, and where theieves break through and steal" (Matthew 6:19), many of us have come to think that a person who tries to build wealth in this life is committing sin. Because Jesus said, "Ye cannot serve God and mammon" (Luke 16:13), we think that pursuing monetary gain compromises our devotion to God. In fact, when Jesus warns against the accumulation of earthly treasures, He is not condemning the idea of making money, He is warning against the danger of allowing money to become one's god.

Preaching about saving and investing money may not be regular Sunday morning material, but that does not mean God

is against it. Truth be told, it is the will of God that you prepare yourself for old age. Remember the industrious ant from
Proverbs 6:6–8? Even Jesus' parable of the unjust steward in
Luke 16:1–13 indirectly provides a lesson on the importance
of planning for the future.

This might sound crude to some readers, but hear me out:
I love God. I love teaching. I love preaching. I want to do it as
long as I have breath in my body. But I want to do it because
I want to, not because I have to. I believe that older people
should work because they want to, not because they have to.

National statistics show that most African-Americans are
deficient in the area of financial investing. One reason for
this is that the church never talks about it. And that is a problem. For many in the African-American community, the
church is the only place where they will ever receive information and instruction on certain subjects. The area of finances happens to be one of those subjects. Consequently, I
am committed to teaching my congregation—and the church
in general—things they need to know for survival in every
aspect of their lives. That is the primary reason behind this
book and, in particular, this chapter on investing.

INVESTING FOR YOUR FUTURE

There is nothing wrong with your money making money.
A person is not pious because he is poor. He is not spiritual
because he is broke. There is nothing inherently wrong about
having Jesus and money.

Let me share a few eye-opening statistics. More than one
half of all households in the United States spend more than
they earn. It does not take a math whiz to see that if you spend
more than you earn, you will have nothing to invest. In 1997,
one half of all families had less than $1,000 in savings. Sadly,

that is a very American phenomenon. According to recent studies, Americans save 4 percent of their disposable income, people in England save 8.7 percent, and people living in Japan save 15.9 percent.

I fall into the baby boomer category (Americans born between 1946–1963). If you're a boomer and make about $50,000 a year, according to current forecasts you will need a million dollars to replace your income in retirement. Retirement age for most boomers will arrive in about twenty years. The future of Social Security continues to hang in doubt, so if we are going to have a million dollars in twenty years, we will need to save $2,000 a month starting today.

The best investment plan is one that will make you the most money on the amount you invest. Just look at your mortgage company's investment plan. They follow this same principle. They invest $200,000 in you and you will earn them $400,000. They double their money by squeezing more money out of you, and then they wait for their stockholders to say, "Well done!" Your credit card company has an investment plan, too. They give you a generous line of credit so that you can spend loads of their money, and then they make triple the amount back from you in interest charges. Then they wait for their stockholders to say, "Well done!"

Both the mortgage company and the credit card company loan you money so that they can take even more money from you over a period of time. Their plan, you see, is to make the most money on their investment. They didn't loan you money because they want to fulfill your dreams. That's just what their advertisements say. Their plan is to invest in you—that is, earn as much money as they can off your need to use their money.

So, how do we escape from dependence on the financial institutions and start doing what they do so that our money can make money for us?

For many people, the simplest and safest way to invest their money is to put it in the bank. Most people wouldn't trust anything else—and there are a lot of folks who don't even trust the bank.

But there is a better way. Table 5.1, which appears at the end of the chapter, shows the growth history of a mutual fund. What is a mutual fund? A mutual fund is an investment portfolio comprised of a diversified selection of shares of stock. A mutual fund pools a large group of investors' money and is controlled by a professional money manager. Though all investments involve some level of risk, mutual funds, if properly diversified, are typically a great way to get the most bang for your buck because of the diversity of stock shares carried under their umbrella. Diversity helps to reduce the risk typically associated with investing in an individual stock or a particular industry. This is why Joe and Mary Member, our "average American family," decided to invest in one.

You remember Joe and Mary Member from chapter 4, right? After paying off all their bills—including their car note and mortgage—they were left with $1,698 per month to invest. If the Members had chosen to put that money under a mattress in 1978, twenty years later they would have saved $407,520. If the Members had taken that money and put it in a savings account at 4 percent fixed interest, twenty years later that account would yield $620,915—clearly a better gain than the mattress! Now, if the Members had purchased a 10-year CD (certificate of deposit) that yields about 10 percent fixed interest, they would have gained $1,235,000—not bad. However, had they invested their money in general mutual funds, which have historically enjoyed returns between 13 and 17 percent, they would have earned $3,231,000. Any questions?

Let me ask you one: Do you think that fifteen or twenty years from now you'll be able to use $3 million? If it's God's will for us to be here that long, most of us would be pleased to have earned that much money for our retirement. But hear this: You're not going to win it in the lottery. And it's not going to fall into your lap. You will have to do something now to achieve that financial goal. You will need to put your money to work. Indeed, the money that you have today can meet you in retirement a thousandfold if you point it in the right direction today. And mutual funds are one reasonably safe way to multiply your money.

MUTUAL EDUCATION

The more you learn about mutual funds and other investment vehicles, the more proficient you will be in putting your money to work. Having the services of a money manager is an excellent course of action, especially for those who do not wish to get their hands too wet in the financial market. A good money manager knows what various investments will yield and is aware of the trends occurring in the market. He can develop a customized portfolio for you that reflects the kind of investments you feel comfortable with and takes into account your desired level of risk.

A good stock portfolio will typically include stocks from a cross section of companies ranging from low to high risk. Generally, this will mean stocks that have performed well in the past, or that have a favorable prognosis to perform well in the future. We're not talking about shares in Joe Willie's Catfish Farm but in companies like Microsoft, AT&T, GM, and Proctor & Gamble.

Just as it's wise to let a trusted money manager advise you on various investment options, it's unwise to blindly invest in a particular stock or mutual fund without personal knowledge of its history, performance, and background. Know exactly where you are investing your money. A few years ago, I preached a sermon on the privatization of the prison system and the questionable business practice of boosting shareholder revenues through a system that promotes the continued disproportionate incarceration of African-American youth. (But that's a subject for another day.) Following that sermon, a member of my congregation approached me. I could see the distress in his eyes as he greeted me. He said, "Pastor, I manage money, and you preached a few weeks ago about the prisons and how much money they're making. Well, the Prison Corporation of America is one of the highest performing stocks we have, and I always encourage people to invest in it. But now my conscience is bothering me, and we need to talk about whether people should invest in prisons." This young man had a problem. His knowledge of how to make the most money suddenly clashed with the Holy Spirit within his soul. In this case, he knew that he could not continue to earn money from a stock that violated his personal ethics. Like him, we all must be wary of investing in companies that might manufacture products or support agendas that conflict with the values God has instilled in us. Our investments must be informed by a vigilant moral and social awareness. Learn to invest your conscience.

To this point, when taken as a whole, there has never been a ten-year period in the history of America that mutual fund investors have lost money. Did you hear what I just said? So, for those readers who experience a phobia about putting their money in anything but a federally insured bank, you might want to consider the track record of mutual funds.

On Table 5.1, the return on Joe and Mary Member's investment at the end of the twenty years is at least 700 percent. Through His parables, Jesus exhorted His people to use their money wisely. In addition to that, the people who used their money the most wisely ended up with the most money.

THE ROAD TO PRAISE

Though Jesus preceded the modern-day stock market by many centuries, He clearly had a good understanding of how it worked. Notice how the rich man in Jesus' parable of the talents diversified. He did not invest all of his money in one place; rather, he spread it out to three different investment vehicles (i.e., servants). In this way risk is reduced, for over time some investments are destined to lose their momentum. But with a diverse investment portfolio, the hope is that stronger-performing investments will make up for the weaker ones at any given time. The rich man also got rid of the investment vehicle that was not earning him an appropriate return and transferred his resources to the vehicles (i.e., servants) that *were* working. You see, Jesus understood the rules of investing. In fact, He wrote the book on them; these are ideas that transcend money and stocks. At their heart, they are spiritual principles—principles of wise stewardship.

In the parable of the talents, the man who buried his money was rebuked for not generating a profit—plus the small amount he did have was taken away from him. His master condemned him as a "wicked and lazy servant." Still, when it comes to managing money, there are two groups of people who are even worse than that lazy servant. They're not mentioned in Matthew 25, but many of us fall into one of those categories. First, there are those who are not saving anything at all. The lazy servant didn't gain any interest off his master's money, but at least he didn't spend what he had. He at least saved the amount that he started with.

And second, there are those who actually make money but give it away in interest. Think of how much more irked that lazy servant's master would have been had the guy taken his one talent, opened up a charge account to supplement it, and then owed fifteen talents. What if instead of taking money and making money, he took the money *and* lost money. That's a sad category to be found in. If God gives you money and you take it, lose it, and then owe more money on top of that, you are indeed an unproductive servant.

And so, we need to ask ourselves which of these undesirable categories we fall into: Are we merely being unproductive with what we have, or worse yet, are we losing even that which we have been given?

If we believe that God is the giver of wealth, then we will want to honor Him with how we handle it. We can exist in a life of bondage to debt, never getting ahead and always at the mercy of other people's resources. Or we can live financially free lives, unfettered by debt and with minds focused on maximizing that which God has given us. If we choose the latter, then we are released to lead lifestyles that honor God through faithful stewardship and grateful praise. The choice is ours.

As you complete this book, if there's someone in the room with you, look at him and say: "The choice is yours. You can get out of debt and into praise." If you're alone as you complete this book, turn your eyes toward heaven and say: "The choice is mine. *I will get out of debt and into praise.*"

Table 5.1
"Hypo" Growth Mutual Fund
Prepared for Joe and Mary Member

Date	Initial Investment	Initial Net Asset Value
6/1/78	$1,698.00	$1,698

Monthly Investments of $1,698.00—Beginning 7/1/78
Dividends and Capital Gains Reinvested

Date	Cumulative Investment	4% Fixed Account Value	10% Fixed Account Value	Mutual Fund Account Value
12/31/78	11,886	12,361	13,075	11,070
12/31/79	32,262	34,047	36,796	42,203
12/31/80	52,638	56,600	62,889	96,902
12/31/81	73,014	80,055	91,591	103,651
12/31/82	93,390	104,448	123,164	160,818
12/31/83	113,766	129,817	157,894	227,542
12/31/84	134,142	156,201	196,097	233,995
12/31/85	154,518	183,640	238,120	341,246
12/31/86	174,894	212,176	284,346	447,282
12/31/87	195,270	241,855	335,194	509,108
12/31/88	215,646	272,720	391,127	587,498
12/31/89	236,022	304,820	452,654	882,112
12/31/90	256,398	338,203	520,332	888,657
12/31/91	276,774	372,923	594,779	1,330,031
12/31/92	297,150	409,030	676,671	1.333,173
12/31/93	317,526	446,583	776,751	1,374,720
12/31/94	337,902	485,637	865,840	1,390,412
12/31/95	358,278	526,253	874,838	1,897,065
12/31/96	378,654	568,495	1,094,735	2,254,429
12/31/97	399,030	612,425	1,226,622	2,862,387
5/31/98	407,520	620,915	1,235,112	3,231,058
Total		620,915	1,235,112	3,231,058

Average annual total return for this illustration: 17.90% (Annual Compounding).
This represents a 700% return on your investment.

FOR
FURTHER STUDY

The material in this book was originally presented as a series of sermons at Salem Baptist Church, 11800 S. Indiana, Chicago, Illinois 60628. An audiotape series of those sermons is available from JTM Ministries P.O. Box 288867 Chicago, 60628 1-866-JTM-3300 under the title *How to Get Out of Debt*, by the Reverend James T. Meeks (Chicago: JTM Ministries, 2000).

Burkett, Larry. *Debt-Free Living*. Revised Edition. Chicago: Moody, 1999.

———. *The Family Financial Workbook: A Practical Guide to Budgeting*. Revised Edition. Chicago, Moody, 2000.

————. *The Financial Guide for the Single Parent.* Revised and Expanded. Chicago: Moody, 1997.

————. *The Financial Guide for the Single Parent.* Workbook. Chicago: Moody, 1997.

————. *How to Manage Your Money Workbook: An In-depth Bible Study on Personal Finances.* Revised Edition. Chicago: Moody, 2000.

————. *Money in Marriage: A Biblical Approach.* Resourceful Living series. Chicago: Moody, 1999.

————. *More Than Finances: A Design for Freedom.* Resourceful Living series. Chicago: Moody, 2000.

————. *The World's Easiest Guide to Finances.* Chicago: Northfield, 2000.

Jenkins, Lee. *Taking Care of Business: Leaving a Financial Legacy for Your Family.* Chicago: Moody, Lift Every Voice, 2001 (forthcoming).

Linder, Ray. *Financial Freedom, Seven Secrets to Reduce Financial Worry.* Chicago: Moody, 1999.

Table 1
Salem Baptist Church Five-Year Debt-Free Program
Financial Plan For _____

Base Margin: _____

Debt Name	Balance	Monthly Payment	Annual Rate	Time to Pay Bills at Monthly Payment	Amount Paid with Payment & Interest	Total Savings When Paid Early	Payoff Date
_____							
_____							
_____							
_____							
_____							
Total							

Principal Formula:
Add:

Once that bill is paid in full
s

Once that bill is paid in full
s

Once that bill is paid in full

Once that bill is paid in full
s

Once that bill is paid

Table 2
Salem Baptist Church Five-Year Debt-Free Program
Financial Plan For _____

Base Margin:

Debt Name	Balance	Monthly Payment	Annual Rate	Time to Pay Bills at Monthly Payment	Amount Paid with Payment & Interest	Total Savings When Paid Early	Payoff Date
Total							

Principal Formula:

Add:

Once that bill is paid in full

s

Once that bill is paid in full

s

Once that bill is paid in full

Once that bill is paid in full

s

Once that bill is paid

Table 3
Salem Baptist Church Five-Year Debt-Free Program
Financial Plan For _____

Base Margin:

Debt Name	Balance	Monthly Payment	Annual Rate	Time to Pay Bills at Monthly Payment	Amount Paid with Payment & Interest	Total Savings When Paid Early	Payoff Date
Total							

Principal Formula:
Add:

Once that bill is paid in full
  s
Once that bill is paid in full
  s
Once that bill is paid in full

Once that bill is paid in full
  s
Once that bill is paid

Table 4
Salem Baptist Church Five-Year Debt-Free Program
Financial Plan For _____

Base Margin:

Debt Name	Balance	Monthly Payment	Annual Rate	Time to Pay Bills at Monthly Payment	Amount Paid with Payment & Interest	Total Savings When Paid Early	Payoff Date
_____							
_____							
_____							
_____							
_____							
Total							

Principal Formula:
Add:

Once that bill is paid in full
    s

Once that bill is paid in full
    s

Once that bill is paid in full

Once that bill is paid in full
    s

Once that bill is paid
    s

Table 5
Salem Baptist Church Five-Year Debt-Free Program
Financial Plan For _____

Base Margin: _____

Debt Name	Balance	Monthly Payment	Annual Rate	Time to Pay Bills at Monthly Payment	Amount Paid with Payment & Interest	Total Savings When Paid Early	Payoff Date
Total							

Principal Formula:
Add:

Once that bill is paid in full

s

Once that bill is paid in full

s

Once that bill is paid in full

Once that bill is paid in full

s

Once that bill is paid

Moody Press, a ministry of Moody Bible Institute,
is designed for education, evangelization, and edification.
If we may assist you in knowing more about Christ
and the Christian life, please write us without obligation:
Moody Press, c/o MLM, Chicago, Illinois 60610.